D1497682

Mysteries
THROUGH
THE AGES

© Aladdin Books Ltd 1996
Designed and produced by
Aladdin Books Ltd
28 Percy Street
London W1P 0LD

First published in the United
States by Copper Beech,
an imprint of
The Millbrook Press
2 Old New Milford Road
Brookfield, Connecticut 06804

Editor: Katie Roden
Design: David West Children's
Book Design
Designer: Flick Killerby
Picture Research:
Brooks Krikler Research
Illustrators: Francis Phillipps,
Rob Shone, Ian Thompson, and
Simon Girling and Associates:
Gary Slater, Stephen Sweet,
and James Field

Printed in Italy

Some of the material in this
book was previously published
in other Aladdin Books series.

Library of Congress Cataloging-in-Publication
Data
Mysteries through the ages/ by Anne Millard ...
[et al.].
p. cm.
Includes index.
Summary: Explores natural and man-made
mysteries of the past in the light of the latest
technology. Includes the Egyptian pyramids, the
dinosaurs, and lost civilizations.
ISBN 0-7613-0518-1 (hardcover)
1. Science--Juvenile literature. 2. Technology--
Juvenile Literature 3. History, Ancient--Juvenile
literature.
[1. Curiosities and wonders. 2. Technology.]
I. Millard, Anne.
Q163.M988 1996   96-13227
031--dc20   CIP
                                        AC

CONTENTS

Mysteries
THROUGH
THE AGES

Written by Anne Millard, Dr. Frances Dipper,
Dr. David Unwin, and Nigel Hawkes

Copper Beech Books
Brookfield, Connecticut

Introduction to
THE MYSTERIES

The Pyramids

The huge pyramids of ancient Egypt are the last surviving wonders of the world. For centuries, their power and mystery have fascinated people, and many attempts have been made to discover their secrets.

Today, with robot cameras and X rays, we are able to understand the pyramids more.

Prehistoric Life

For centuries, people have discovered strange bones and fossils above and below the Earth's surface, but it is only recently that scientists have begun to investigate their origins. We are now able to understand the origins of life on Earth, from microscopic organisms to the largest dinosaurs, and from the first mammals to earliest humans. However, there are still many puzzles to solve.

The Universe

Since the 17th-century when astronomers built the first telescopes, we have been able to explore the mysteries of space. Today, however, we have more advanced scientific inventions, such as space probes and satellites, which help us to understand more of the universe which surrounds our planet.

Lost Civilizations

Steeped in legend and rumors, the world's lost places and people have intrigued archaeologists for thousands of years, and many attempts have been made to unravel their mysteries. These days we are able to piece together the clues to their existence, and so to discover whether they existed in the real world as well as in books and legends.

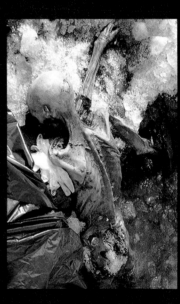

The Ocean Deep

The power and mystery of our oceans has fascinated people for ages, and many attempts have been made to discover their secrets. Now, thanks to modern technology such as robot submarines, radar, and underwater cameras, we are able to comprehend the watery depths more. Yet there are still many questions left unanswered. This book explores *all* these mysteries and more, using modern science, myths and legends, and recent discoveries. It may help *you* to solve them yourself.

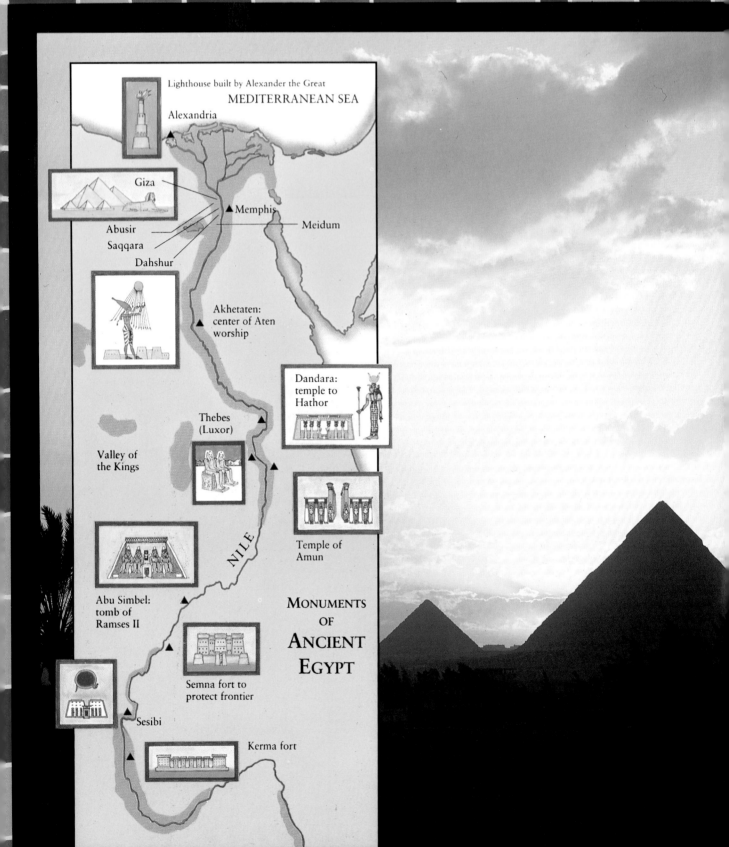

Lighthouse built by Alexander the Great

MEDITERRANEAN SEA

Alexandria

Giza

▲ Memphis

Abusir

Saqqara

Meidum

Dahshur

Akhetaten:
center of Aten
worship

Dandara:
temple to
Hathor

Thebes
(Luxor)

Valley of
the Kings

Temple of
Amun

NILE

Abu Simbel:
tomb of
Ramses II

MONUMENTS
OF
ANCIENT
EGYPT

Semna fort to
protect frontier

Sesibi

Kerma fort

Chapter One
THE PYRAMIDS

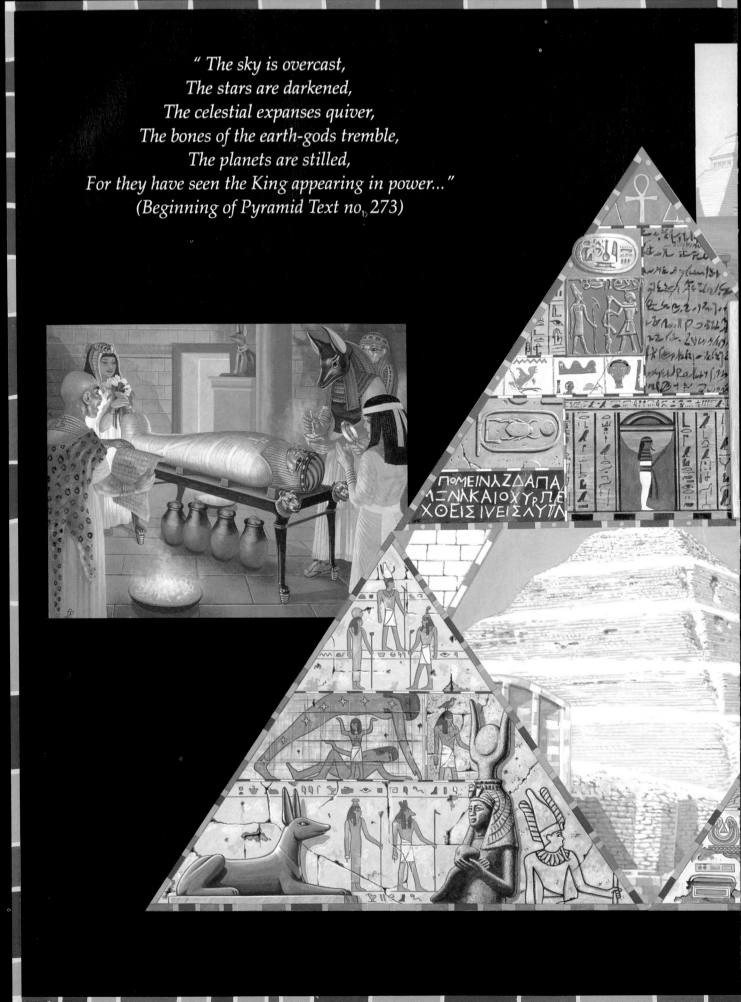

" The sky is overcast,
The stars are darkened,
The celestial expanses quiver,
The bones of the earth-gods tremble,
The planets are stilled,
For they have seen the King appearing in power..."
(Beginning of Pyramid Text no. 273)

Introduction to THE PYRAMIDS

They stand silent and mysterious on the Giza Plateau in Egypt – three mighty pyramids and six smaller ones. Meanwhile, across the world, vast pyramidlike structures tower above the rainforests of Central and South America – monuments of great empires which now have disappeared.

There are more than three dozen kings' pyramids in Egypt, but as time passed, all knowledge of their royal history was lost. People came up with some weird ideas, believing that the pyramids were anything from ancient observatories to the work of visitors from outer space!

It was not until the nineteenth century A.D. that the pyramids were examined in great detail. Since the age of the first explorers, lots of puzzles have been solved, but modern science still cannot explain many unanswered questions. In the last few years, a French and a Japanese team have both claimed to have evidence that there are other chambers in the Great Pyramid at Giza, unopened since the days of Khufu over 4,000 years ago. What secrets might these chambers reveal? Will they help us to understand the great civilization of ancient Egypt?

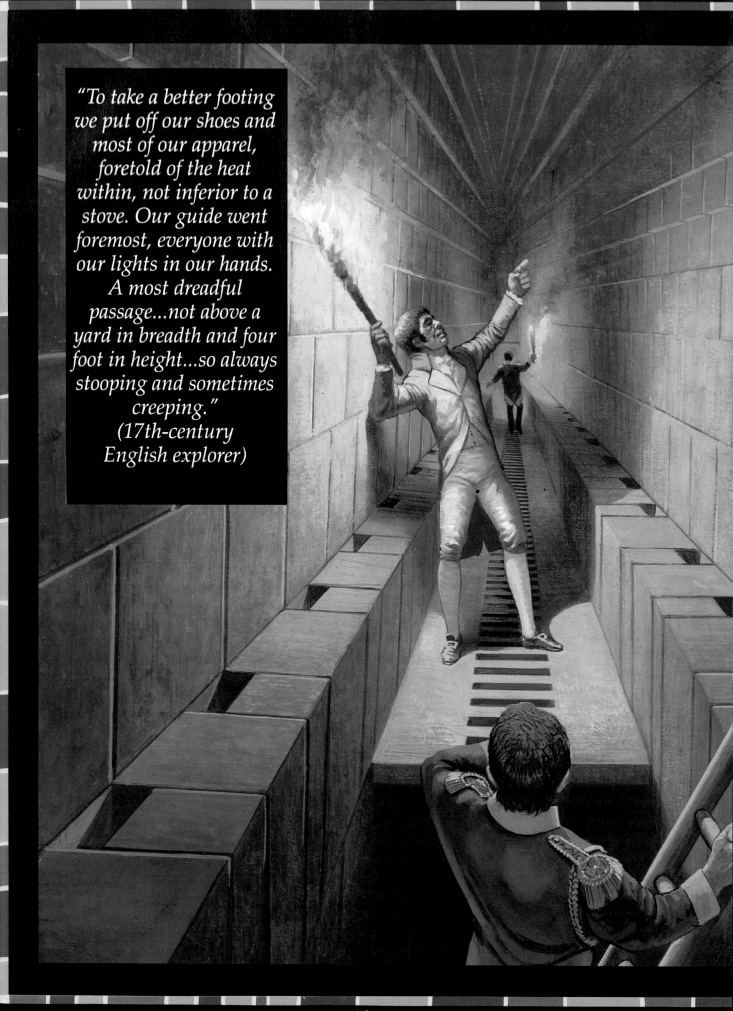

"To take a better footing we put off our shoes and most of our apparel, foretold of the heat within, not inferior to a stove. Our guide went foremost, everyone with our lights in our hands. A most dreadful passage...not above a yard in breadth and four foot in height...so always stooping and sometimes creeping."
(17th-century English explorer)

The First EXPLORERS

If you visit a pyramid today, you will find electric lights, steps to climb, and handrails to help you find your way. When early explorers entered 300 years ago, they had only flickering candlelight and the strong hands of their guides to lead them into the intense heat and fearsome darkness of the pyramids. There was a terrible stench, and the air was dusty. But the explorers braved the heat and lack of light, and had many adventures!

The first tourists to visit the Giza pyramids were the ancient Egyptians themselves, then the Greeks and Romans. After the Arab invasion of Egypt in A.D. 639, the outer stones from the pyramids were used to build the city of Cairo. For centuries after, very few people visited Egypt, so scholars had very little information about the pyramids. Were these wonderful monuments just tombs? Surely they must have had other uses?

Early Explorers
AND DISCOVERERS

Throughout history, people have tried to understand the pyramids. Early Christians thought they were places where priests watched the stars. In the nineteenth century, some people believed that the measurements of the Great Pyramid were inspired by God, and that from them they could predict the future! But by then, scholars could read ancient Egyptian writing and they had started to dig up historic sites. The pyramids were finally known as the last resting places of Egypt's ancient kings.

A SENSITIVE APPROACH
Sir William Flinders Petrie (1852-1942) is regarded as the father of modern archaeology. He dug sites carefully, recorded everything in detail, and published his results. His first job in Egypt was to measure the Great Pyramid.

EARLY ADVENTURER
Jean de Thevenot (below) was one of the first explorers of ancient Egyptian sites.

THE BURIED SPHINX
In Egyptian legend, the Sphinx (the statue which guards the pyramids) appeared to a prince in a dream. It promised to make him king if he cleared away the sand from its body. He did so, and became Tuthmose IV.

NAPOLÉON'S NIGHTMARE
Napoléon Bonaparte, the Emperor of France, led an invasion of Egypt in 1798. Legend has it that he ventured into the Great Pyramid alone, only to emerge pale, shaken, and gasping for air. What secrets did he encounter in the darkness? We will never know...

Treasure hunters

In the early nineteenth century, great damage was done by collectors and their agents. They entered the tombs in all sorts of ways, including blasting their way in! Giovanni Belzoni was a former circus strongman, who was hired by a collector to gather ancient Egyptian artifacts. He had no idea of preservation – one of his writings describes how he clumsily crushed Late-Period mummies as he forced his way into a tomb.

Preserving the treasures

Many museums and universities have carried out excavations in Egypt. The objects found are treated by experts, then stored for future research. X rays, medical scanners (below), robot photography, and many other modern techniques are used to help scientists understand the secrets of the tombs.

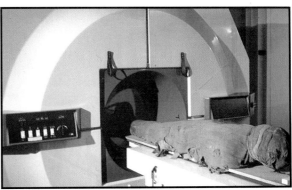

Pyramid graffiti

Belzoni even carved his name on the stones of the pyramids!

When did tourists start to arrive? In 1869, Thomas Cook, a British travel agent, bought a steamboat in Egypt and offered a new service – a package holiday. He charged one amount to cover everything – travel to Egypt, a cruise along the Nile, and a guide. Until then, visitors to Egypt had to arrange all these details for themselves, which could be both difficult and extremely expensive.

Uncharted territory

After the Arab invasion of Egypt, few people were able to visit the country. Little was known about the pyramids, the Nile Valley and its surroundings, or the culture and history of ancient Egypt.

Reading the
HIEROGLYPHS

The Egyptians had invented a picture writing that we call hieroglyphs by about 3000 B.C. Some of their signs were single letters; others had the value of two, three, or more letters. These were combined to form words. Hieroglyphs take a long time to write, so the Egyptians invented a "shorthand" script which we call *hieratic*, and another, *demotic*, about 2,500 years later. These were used in daily life, and hieroglyphs were kept for religious texts only. For centuries, no one could read the hieroglyphs, but in 1822 a great breakthrough was made...

THE ROYAL CARTOUCHE
To emphasize and protect royal or holy names, the Egyptians wrote them in a frame called a cartouche *(above). Champollion (see below) used cartouches on the Rosetta Stone to help him translate the hieroglyphs. He read the one below in its Greek version. It was Ptolemy, a ruler of Egypt. He then worked out which hieroglyphs spelled the name.*

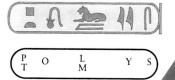

| P | | O | | L | Y | S |
| T | | | M | | | |

* no translation

	i	y	y	*
w	*	b	p	f
m	n	r	h	
h	kh	h(soft)	s	s
sh	q	k	g(hard)	
t	tj	d	dj	

FINDING THE KEY
The Rosetta Stone is carved in hieroglyphs, demotic and Greek. It was discovered in Egypt in 1799.

ΠΟΜΕΙΝΑΖΔΑΠΑ
ΛΞΝΛΚΑΙΟΧΥΡΠΕ
ΧΘΕΙΣΙΝΕΙΣΛΥΤΛ

CRACKING THE CODE
In 1822, a brilliant young French scholar, named Jean François Champollion, used his knowledge of ancient Greek to read the Rosetta Stone. At last, the mysterious hieroglyphs could be translated.

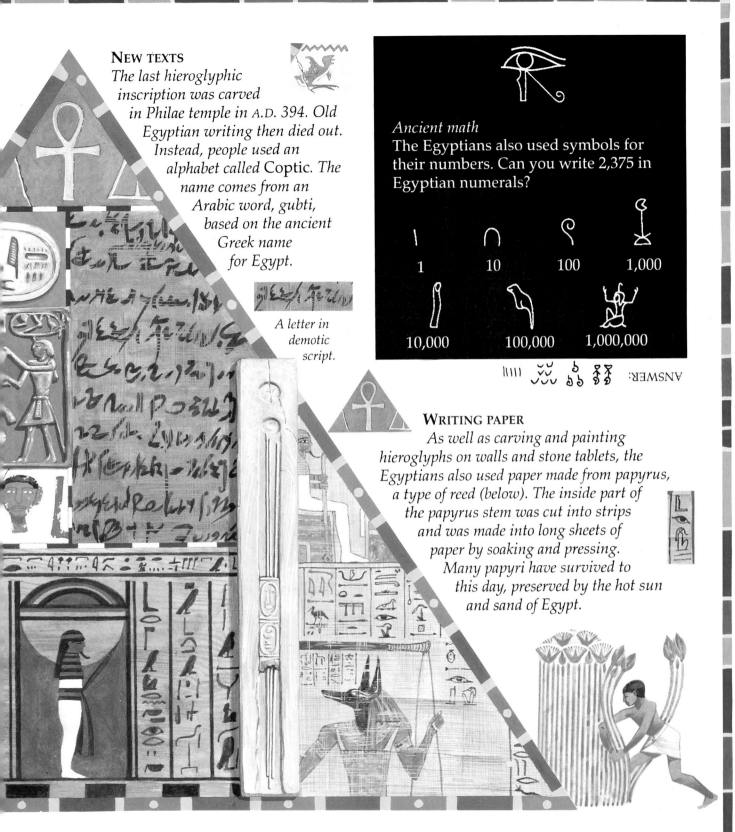

NEW TEXTS

The last hieroglyphic inscription was carved in Philae temple in A.D. 394. Old Egyptian writing then died out. Instead, people used an alphabet called **Coptic**. The name comes from an Arabic word, *gubti*, based on the ancient Greek name for Egypt.

A letter in demotic script.

Ancient math

The Egyptians also used symbols for their numbers. Can you write 2,375 in Egyptian numerals?

1	10	100	1,000
10,000	100,000	1,000,000	

ANSWER:

WRITING PAPER

As well as carving and painting hieroglyphs on walls and stone tablets, the Egyptians also used paper made from papyrus, a type of reed (below). The inside part of the papyrus stem was cut into strips and was made into long sheets of paper by soaking and pressing. Many papyri have survived to this day, preserved by the hot sun and sand of Egypt.

HEAVENLY GUIDE BOOKS

In the pyramid of the last king of Dynasty V and in all Dynasty VI pyramids, we find writings called **the Pyramid Texts**. These were believed to help the king move easily into the next world (heaven).

They contained prayers, pleas, and ritual pronouncements to the gods. It was hoped that the gods, such as Anubis (left), would welcome the king and allow him to pass into the next world to live a new, happy, and everlasting life.

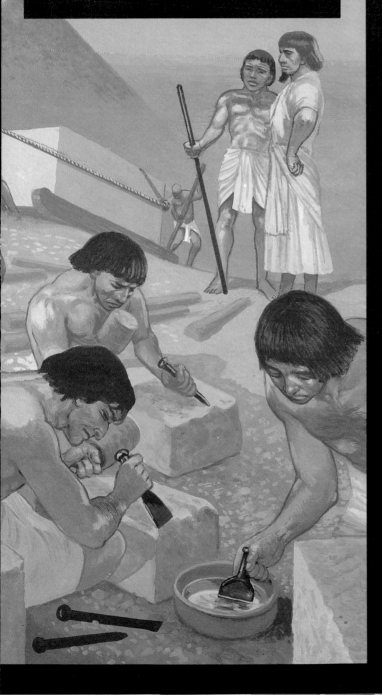

Building the PYRAMIDS

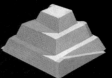

Why were the pyramids built? Who built them? How was it done? These questions puzzled the world for centuries, even after Champollion translated the hieroglyphs. It was then clear that the pyramids were tombs. The names of the kings who had them built are inscribed or painted in the tombs, mixed with the names of the groups of workers who built them.

Most Egyptian people were farmers. Egypt has very little rain, but water is supplied by the Nile. Every year the river flooded, covering the land for four months. During this time, the *Inundation*, the farmers could not tend their fields, so the king summoned them to work on his pyramid instead. This labor was a form of tax to the king. People usually went willingly, although the work was hard. They believed that the king was a god and would look after them in the next world in return for their labor.

Construction AND LABOR

BUILDING BLOCKS
Most of the stone for the pyramids came from local quarries, but the fine white limestone for the casing (right) came from Tura on the east bank of the Nile, and had to be floated across the river. Each block was then put on a wooden sled and dragged into place by a group of workers. To help the sled run smoothly, the workers put wooden rollers on the ground in front of it. Water was poured continuously on to the rollers, so that the heat and friction caused by the movement of the enormous stone would not start a fire.

When a suitable, firm site had been chosen, the ground was flattened and the base of the pyramid was stretched out. Building could then begin. The great stones were tied to sleds and dragged into place, one at a time, by teams of workers. Finally, a white limestone casing was put on the pyramid.

THE CONSTRUCTION SITE
Even straight-sided pyramids were built with a step pyramid inside them (top). To build the central structure, the stone blocks were probably dragged into place up ramps made of bricks and rubble (center). One wide ramp (bottom) was used to add the outer casing. It was made longer and higher as the pyramid grew taller, and was taken apart when building ended.

How many blocks made a pyramid?
This depended on its size. The Great Pyramid contains about 2,300,000.
How much did each block weigh?
This also depended on size. Most Great Pyramid blocks were about 2.5 tons.

THE HOLY ARCHITECT
The designer of the first pyramid was named Imhotep. In about 2700 B.C., he built a step pyramid for King Zoser. He was so wise, and his pyramid was so impressive, that he was later worshiped as a god!

The pyramid complex

On the edge of a complex was the Valley Temple, which was probably where the king's body was prepared for burial. A causeway (path) led to a Mortuary Temple, where offerings were made to the king's spirit. There was also a small pyramid for the queen and rectangular tombs, or mastabas, for the royal family and the courtiers.

Mortuary Temple

Causeway

Valley Temple

GLEAMING WHITE
Originally, the pyramids were covered with fine white limestone (above). However, over the centuries this was stolen.

A HUGE WORKFORCE
Skilled stone masons, laborers and other craftspeople worked all year round on a pyramid, but most of the work was done during the four months of the Inundation, when the farmers arrived to do their labor tax. They were fed, housed, and clothed by the king. It was an enormous feat to look after so many people – as many as 80,000 at one time – and to organize their work efficiently! The workers were paid in beer, oil, and linen. They also received food including meat, fish, vegetables, fruit, cheese, and a type of wholewheat bread.

TOOLS OF THE TRADE
The Old Kingdom pyramid builders had copper chisels and saws, and wooden sleds to pull the blocks. To carve the blocks from the quarries, wooden wedges were driven into the rock and soaked with water. The wood swelled, splitting the stone. Another method was to heat the rock then throw cold water over it, to make it crack.

P y r a m i d s
AND KINGS

Egypt's kings were believed to be related to the gods and were treated with great respect. At first they were buried in rectangular brick tombs. But Imhotep decided that mud did not last long enough for royal burials, and built a stone mastaba for his ruler, Zoser. He made it bigger by putting another mastaba on top, then another and another...and the world's first step pyramid was born. King Huni built another step pyramid, but his son Sneferu made its sides straight.
From then on, all pyramids were built with straight sides.

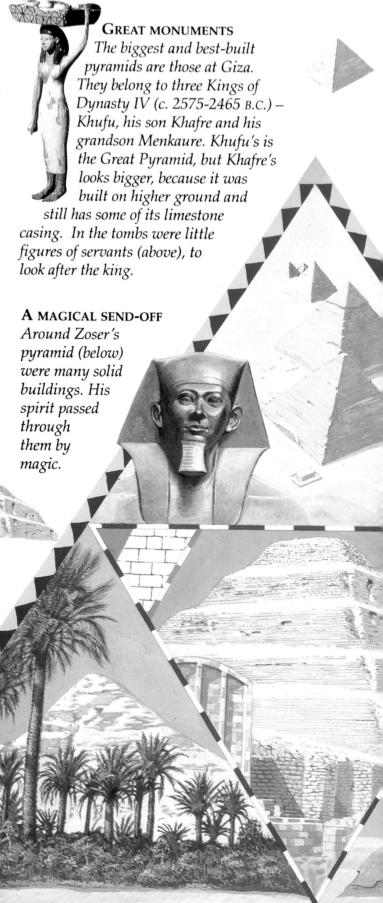

GREAT MONUMENTS
The biggest and best-built pyramids are those at Giza. They belong to three Kings of Dynasty IV (c. 2575-2465 B.C.) – Khufu, his son Khafre and his grandson Menkaure. Khufu's is the Great Pyramid, but Khafre's looks bigger, because it was built on higher ground and still has some of its limestone casing. In the tombs were little figures of servants (above), to look after the king.

A MAGICAL SEND-OFF
Around Zoser's pyramid (below) were many solid buildings. His spirit passed through them by magic.

THE ROYAL GRAVEYARD
The smaller, less well-built pyramids at Abusir and Saqqara belong to the kings of Dynasties V and VI. These sites are packed full of tombs, dating from throughout the Egyptian period. The tombs include the pyramid of King Userkaf (right), with a colossal head of the ruler.

20

Did the pyramids ever go wrong?
The pyramid builders were usually incredibly accurate, down to the last inch. But everyone makes mistakes! King Sneferu built two pyramids at Dahshur, one of which is known as the Bent Pyramid. It was meant to have straight sides, but when it had been partially built, the architects decided that its sides were too steep and it might collapse. It was therefore finished with the sides sloping more gently at the bottom, so it looks bent.

A COMPLETE DISASTER

The Meidum Pyramid was the engineers' biggest blunder! At some point, all the outer casing fell off, dragging most of the insides down with it. Sneferu's engineers made a mistake – they built the new, straight-sided casing on a foundation of soft sand instead of rock.

The Bent Pyramid at Dahshur

Zoser (right), a god-king of Egypt

A class of its own

The Great Pyramid is unlike any other pyramid, with three main chambers rather than one. Were these last-minute changes of design to trick grave robbers? The highest chamber is the only burial chamber, where the king lay.

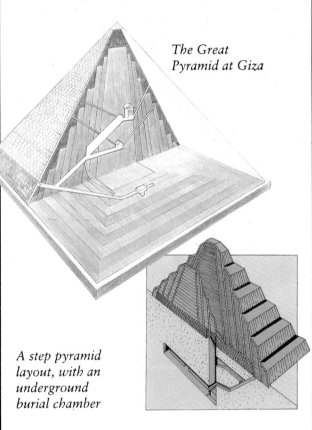

The Great Pyramid at Giza

A step pyramid layout, with an underground burial chamber

The lower one is called the "Queen's Chamber," although the queen was buried in her own small pyramid. There are four tiny shafts in the king's and queen's chambers. Many people think they were built to help the royal spirits reach the stars. Most other pyramids are simpler, with one central burial chamber and two or three antechambers.

"Oh King, you have not departed dead, you have departed alive!...Raise yourself up, oh King! Receive your head, collect your bones, gather your limbs together..."
(Pyramid Text)

A Life after DEATH

The Egyptians believed that the only way they could properly enjoy life in the next world was if their bodies survived. Even the king's body had to last, in case he needed it, although his soul traveled to the next world to live with his godly relatives.

In Egypt, people had been buried in shallow graves in the hot desert sand. This dried and preserved their bodies in a natural way. However, once the Egyptians put their kings and nobles in splendid tombs, the bodies decayed easily, and artificial ways of preserving them were invented. The most successful method – mummification – was at its peak in the New Kingdom. The internal organs (lungs, brain, liver etc.) were taken out and the body was covered with a salt called *natron*, which dried it out. It was then stuffed with linen and resin (the sap from trees), and wrapped in hundreds of yards of linen bandages. Many bodies are still almost perfectly preserved today.

Preparing for THE AFTERLIFE

It sometimes seems that the ancient Egyptians spent most of their time thinking about death, but this isn't true. They loved their life on Earth so much that they believed the next world would be like Egypt, but without sadness, worries, or suffering. They therefore went to great trouble to prepare for their eternal life and to make sure they would have a good time. This meant building a comfortable tomb, full of all the furniture and belongings they might need. Over all, they made sure they would have regular supplies of food, drink, and entertainment.

SOULS AND SPIRITS
The Egyptians believed they had three spirits – the ka, ba, and akh. The ka was the life force of a person. After death it lived in the tomb, and was kept comfortable with offerings and servants (right). The ba represented the personality. It was shown as a human-headed bird, but it could change shape and leave the tomb. The akh, written as a crested ibis, went to join the stars, or Osiris.

MEMORY AIDS
Mummies were decorated with an image of the dead, so the ba recognized the body. Mirrors and combs enabled the dead to look their best.

HEAVENLY PLEASURES
Paintings of food and entertainers (below) were often placed in tombs, to keep the souls happy.

Why are mummies called mummies?
The Arabs thought bitumen was used in embalming, so called mummies after their word for bitumen, "mummiya."

WEALTH AND RICHES
Jewelry and treasures were usually put in the tombs of both men and women. Even the poorest people were buried with some jewelry, to make sure they looked impressive in their new life with the gods and goddesses.

HEAVENLY SERVANTS
Little servant figures, or shabtis (right), were put in the tombs to do the dead person's work in the next world.

Grave robbers

Everyone knew that great riches were placed in royal tombs. While guards watched over the burial places, these treasures were safe. But over the centuries the tombs were no longer guarded, and thieves broke in – even though they knew it insulted the gods. If they were caught, they would be executed, but this did not put them away!

LONG LIFE
The organs were preserved and put in containers called canopic jars.

SAILING IN THE SKY
In some dynasties, model boats were placed in the tombs. They represented the boat that carried dead people across the Nile to the next world.

Full-sized boats have been found in several tombs at Giza. They were probably used by the king in life, and to carry his dead body over the Nile to his final resting place.

Joining the GODS

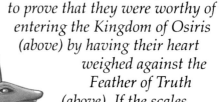

In the Old Kingdom, the chief god was the sun god Re, who sailed across the sky every day in a boat. His children were Tefnut (Moisture) and Shu (Air). They were the parents of Geb (Earth) and Nut (Sky), whose children were Osiris, Set (the lord of desert and storms), Nephthys his wife, and the stars. Set murdered his brother Osiris, cut up his body and threw the pieces into the Nile. Isis and Nephthys gathered up the pieces and brought Osiris back to life, with the help of Anubis. When a king died, he went to the heavens to join the gods.

WEIGHING YOUR CHANCES
Anubis (below) was the guardian of the dead. He held the scales of justice. People had to prove that they were worthy of entering the Kingdom of Osiris (above) by having their heart weighed against the Feather of Truth (above). If the scales balanced, a person had led a good life. An evil heart would tip the scales and they would be thrown to a terrible monster, the Devourer.

IMAGES OF THE GODS
Gods like Geb (bottom center) and Shu (above right) were believed to have beards. Kings, and queens if they ruled as kings, wore false beards to show their closeness to the gods.

Which deity had the most power? Isis, the loving mother of all, had more magic power than any other god or goddess. In ancient Roman times, her fame spread outside Egypt – evidence of Isis worship has been found as far north as Hadrian's Wall, in England, built in about A.D. 120.

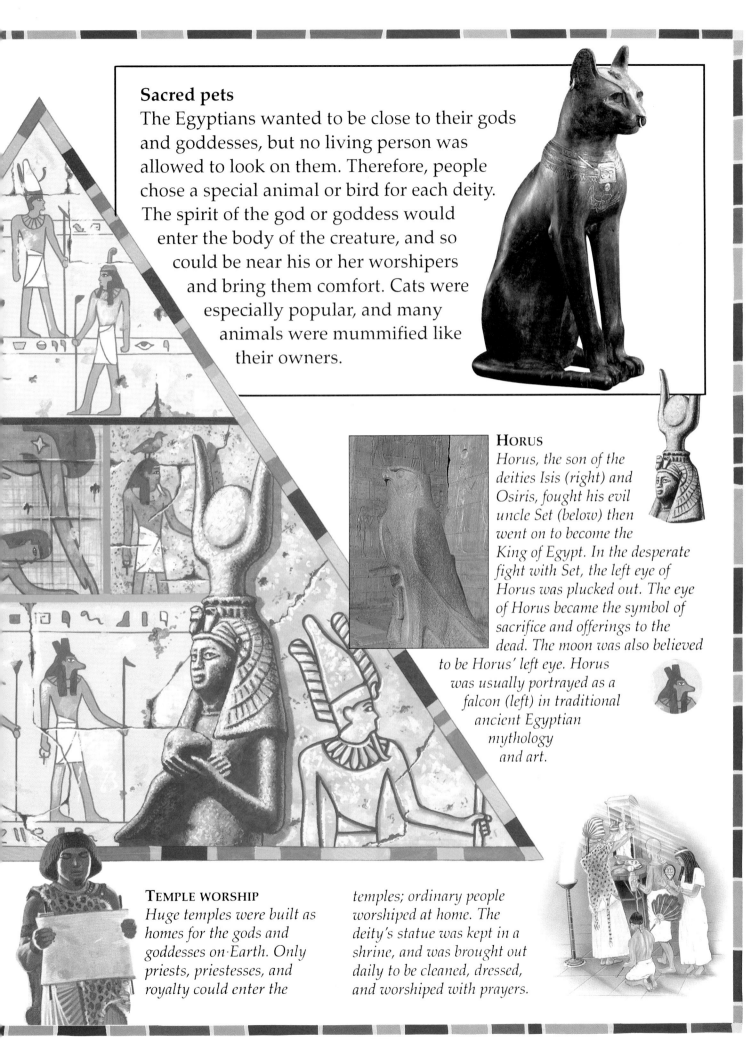

Sacred pets

The Egyptians wanted to be close to their gods and goddesses, but no living person was allowed to look on them. Therefore, people chose a special animal or bird for each deity. The spirit of the god or goddess would enter the body of the creature, and so could be near his or her worshipers and bring them comfort. Cats were especially popular, and many animals were mummified like their owners.

HORUS

Horus, the son of the deities Isis (right) and Osiris, fought his evil uncle Set (below) then went on to become the King of Egypt. In the desperate fight with Set, the left eye of Horus was plucked out. The eye of Horus became the symbol of sacrifice and offerings to the dead. The moon was also believed to be Horus' left eye. Horus was usually portrayed as a falcon (left) in traditional ancient Egyptian mythology and art.

TEMPLE WORSHIP

Huge temples were built as homes for the gods and goddesses on Earth. Only priests, priestesses, and royalty could enter the temples; ordinary people worshiped at home. The deity's statue was kept in a shrine, and was brought out daily to be cleaned, dressed, and worshiped with prayers.

"A stairway to the sky is set up for me that I may ascend to the sky..."

"May the sky make the sunlight strong for you, may you rise up to the sky..."

(Pyramid Texts 284, 523)

New Ideas and INVESTIGATIONS

The pyramid was the place where the king's body and possessions were buried, and where offerings were supposed to be made to him forever. But it was also the place where the god-king's spirit was launched to the heavens to join his relatives, the gods and goddesses.

Most experts agree that the souls of the early kings were believed to be heading for the stars. Step pyramids were stairways to the stars, and straight-sided pyramids were like sunbeams made of stone, which the king could climb to reach Re.

But the pyramids may have had many more uses. Does the pyramid also represent a mound, which in Egyptian creation stories was the first land to appear from the original nothingness? Does the layout of the Giza pyramids imitate the position of the main stars that form the belt of the groups we call Orion and Sirius? How can we explain several missing mummies and empty tombs?

Secrets of THE STARS

The movements of the sun, moon, and stars were important in Egyptian religion, and their calendar was based on these movements. Each week was marked by a new group of stars rising in the sky at dawn. The Egyptians divided the stars into constellations (groups), but their groupings were different from ours. Maps of the heavens show the sun-god and stars crossing the sky in boats. This shows the importance of the Nile to the Egyptians.

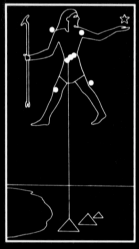

MAPPING THE STARS
The group of stars we call "Orion" was known as "Sahu" by the Egyptians. They believed that the soul of Osiris went there after he was murdered by his brother, Set. Near Orion is the star we call Sirius, known to the Egyptians as Sopdet. They saw Sopdet as Isis, the wife of Osiris. Sopdet spends seventy days a year below the horizon, invisible from Egypt. Its return to view marked the Egyptian New Year. The Nile flood came at that time, and was believed to be Isis weeping for Osiris.

STARRY GODS
Many temples were decorated with constellation gods (right) and star deities.

HEAVENLY BIRDS
In the Old Kingdom, swallows were identified with the stars. They heralded the dawn, and were often shown on the front of Re's sun-boat. In later images, the head of a falcon was often shown descending from the sky. It represented the sun's rays, and the eye of Horus.

HOLY COW
The cow (right) was the sacred animal of the goddess Hathor, the Queen of Heaven.

How did the Egyptian calendar work? The Egyptian week had ten days. Three weeks made a month and twelve months a year. There were five holy days at the end of the year, making 365 days.

THE SACRED SKY
The sky hieroglyph (above) shows the heavens as a solid ceiling, and was often used above doorways.

A VIEW OF THE WORLD
The sun was believed to be the right eye of the god Horus.

THE LOVE OF THE GODS
The Egyptians believed that the sky was the goddess Nut (below), stretching her body over the Earth. In Egyptian mythology, Nut married Geb, the earth god, but Re was against their marriage and ordered their father, Shu, to push them apart. However, by this time Geb and Nut were already the parents of the stars and of the four great deities.

Mysteries of the heavens
What are the four narrow shafts that lead out of the burial chambers in Khufu's pyramid? Recently, it was discovered that one of the two shafts in the king's chamber points to the northern stars, which never sink below the horizon. The other points to Orion. Was this a passage for the dead king's soul to reach Osiris quickly? It is also suggested that the queen's chamber shafts point to the stars. One faces Sirius – could this be another passageway to the heavens?

Orion/
Sahu/
Osiris

Sirius/
Sopdet/
Isis

The Giza pyramids are not quite in a straight line. The Egyptologist Robert Bauval claims they are laid out like the three main stars of Orion/Sahu/Osiris and that they were built for astronomical as well as religious reasons.

THE DIVINE STARS
The northern stars were always visible, so were named "The Imperishable Ones."

Puzzles and MYSTERIES

In the Middle Ages (A.D. 1100-1500), the pyramids were said to have been grain stores, then were believed to be early observatories. In the nineteenth century, one theory said that the Great Pyramid's measurements were inspired by God and contained a code that could predict all the main events of world history! Even today, crazy ideas about the pyramids are still popular, but new evidence and theories are constantly improving our understanding of these great, mysterious monuments.

A SECRET CHAMBER?

In 1994, a team of scientists sent a tiny robot, called UPUAUT II, up the narrow southern shaft of the queen's chamber of Khufu's pyramid. They wanted to see if they could ventilate the pyramid better, because of the number of tourists visiting it every year. The robot traveled about 200 feet...then its TV camera showed a slab of stone with copper handles blocking its way. What lies behind this tiny door? Could there be a room? What might it contain – a statue, hidden writings, wonderful treasures...or nothing at all? Archaeologists are hoping to look through a crack at the base of the stone with a tiny camera, the kind used by doctors to see inside patients. What will it reveal?

AN ANCIENT PUZZLE

Archaeologists believe that the Sphinx was carved from stone left in a quarry when the pyramids were completed. But there is a theory that it is thousands of years older than the pyramids, because the wind and rain have worn away its face much more than the surface of the pyramids. It is believed that the Sphinx was the work of an earlier civilization. This is extremely unlikely because no other traces of such a civilization have been found.

EXTRATERRESTRIAL EGYPTIANS

There are even people who suggest that the pyramids were built by aliens!

THE CASE OF THE MISSING MUMMY

When excavators entered the unfinished step pyramid of King Sekhemkhet, the stones blocking the passage were in place, a wreath of flowers was still on the coffin and the lid was sealed. Excitedly, they pried it open, and found...nothing! What had happened to the body? Had it been buried secretly somewhere else, to fool robbers? Had it been stolen? Or had it never been buried at all? So far, the mummy has still not been found, and it is unlikely that it ever will. It seems that the pyramids will present us with new puzzles and mysteries forever.

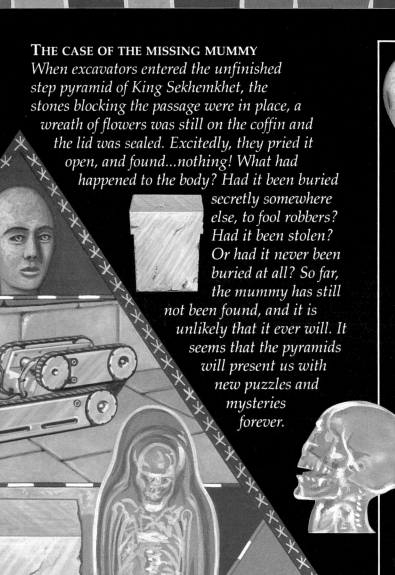

Hi-tech research

In recent years, science and technology have helped archaeologists to unravel many of the mysteries of Egypt. There are many ways of dating human and animal remains, wood, and pottery. X rays have been used to examine mummies for many years, and modern medical scanners can give an even better picture of what is inside them. This is very important, because unwrapping a mummy can destroy it. Artists and computers can reconstruct the faces of people who lived 3,000 years ago.

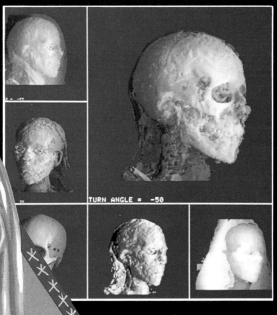

TURN ANGLE = -50

What did the Egyptians look like? Archaeologists use police techniques

to recreate mummies' faces from ancient skulls, using clay.

"The usual method of sacrifice was to open the victim's chest, pull out his heart while he was still half alive, and then knock down the man, rolling him down the temple steps which were awash with blood."
(José de Acosta, 1590)

Pyramids around THE WORLD

The Egyptians were not the only civilization to build great pyramid-shaped structures. The ancient peoples of Mesopotamia (now eastern Syria, southeastern Turkey, and most of Iraq) built pyramid shapes to bring them closer to their gods and goddesses. They constructed mud-brick platforms, with temples to house the gods on the flat tops. There the priests sent offerings and prayers to the gods. We call these temple platforms *ziggurats*.

In North, Central, and South America, peoples such as the Aztecs and Incas also built flat-topped pyramids (left). People were sometimes buried under them, but they were not meant to be tombs. Temples were built on top of these pyramids, where sacrifices of food, animals, and sometimes human beings were offered. Early Native American peoples built large, pyramid-shaped mounds in which to bury their dead and to use as shrines.

Popular PYRAMIDS

Central and South America saw the rise and fall of many civilizations, such as the Olmecs, Toltecs, Maya, Incas, and Aztecs, before the arrival of European settlers in the sixteenth century. These peoples first built great mounds of earth, then developed flat-topped pyramids by casing the mounds in stone with steep steps. These were places where gods and people could meet. The pyramids had temples on top, but some had burials underneath. The Europeans destroyed hundreds of ancient cities, and many treasures and artifacts were lost.

SACRIFICE AND CEREMONY

To please their gods, the Maya offered their own blood at special ceremonies. Sometimes they also offered human lives. The Aztecs believed that their many gods needed human hearts to stay strong, and sacrificed thousands of people to them. Sacrifices were made before shrines on flat-topped pyramids, like that at Tikal in Guatemala (right). Picture writing has been found on some Mayan pyramids, and is now being translated.

INCA PYRAMID MOUNDS

The Incas ruled a vast area of South America in the fifteenth century. In the city of Cuzco in Peru they built a great temple called the Coricancha (right) to their sun-god, Inti. There they offered food and beer and sacrificed animals to their god.

THE MODERN MONUMENT

A glass pyramid (right) is the entrance to the Louvre Museum in Paris.

Did other people mummify their dead?
Mummification is a very old practice in South America. Mummies of the Nazca people in Peru date from about 200 B.C. to A.D. 500. Human sacrifices were sometimes buried in the Andean mountains, where they were naturally preserved in the snow and ice.

REMEMBERING THE DEAD

Stone or ceramic funeral masks were used in the traditional funeral rites of several Native American cultures, similar to that of the Egyptians.

NORTH AMERICA
Some Native North American people also built pyramids. The Mississippians built towns in A.D. 700-1500. The important buildings were set on great mounds of earth (above). Many peoples buried their dead in earth mounds with gifts and treasure.

A lasting impression
In modern times, architects have used pyramid shapes and Egyptian decorations as part of their designs. For example, the casino based on the Great Pyramid which was built in Las Vegas. It is the same size as Khufu's tomb, and is guarded by a giant Sphinx! Decorations, such as those on the Empire State Building or these apartments in San Francisco (below), are directly influenced by Egyptian pyramid paintings, while tiles and decorations often show decorative papyrus-leaf designs.

BIBLICAL BUILDINGS
The early people of Mesopotamia built mud-brick temples on platforms on the ruins of older temples. The platforms grew taller over the years and became huge, stepped mounds similar to early pyramids.

We call them ziggurats. The great ziggurat Etemenanki was built by Nebuchadnezzar (604-561 B.C.) in Babylon, home of the famous Hanging Gardens. It might have given rise to the story of the Tower of Babel (right).

The Lasting
I M A G E

A LASTING FASHION
Middle Kingdom rulers also had pyramids, which were usually made of brick rather than stone. People realized that pyramids were easily robbed, so the New Kingdom rulers picked a remote valley to hide their rock-cut tombs – the Valley of the Kings, it has a pyramid-shaped mountain towering above it. The workers who cut the rock built their own village at Deir-el-Medina. All their tombs had mini pyramids on top.

After Napoléon's expedition in 1798, a craze for ancient Egypt began. This happened again after the opening of the Suez Canal in 1869, and in 1922 with the discovery of the tomb of Tutankhamen. Each time, people collected Egyptian antiques and visited Egypt. Others bought Egyptian-style jewelry, furniture, architecture, or ornaments. Egyptian images were used in all types of advertisements – even for things that had nothing to do with Egypt. Egyptian decorations are still used in many products, from chocolate to makeup.

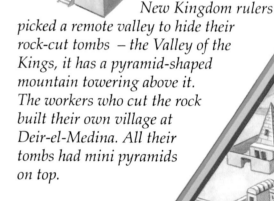

Is the Great Pyramid great? The sides are 229 yards long, and the height just over 145 yards. The base is so big that you could easily fit 8 football fields onto it.

WHAT WERE THEY FOR?

A mosaic in St. Mark's Cathedral in Venice, Italy, shows how people in the Middle Ages continued to be fascinated by the pyramids. They were believed to be ancient grain stores built by Joseph (of multi-colored coat fame), and were shown complete with doors and windows!

GRUESOME USES

In medieval Europe, many people believed that mummies had healing powers. They ground them into fine powder, for medicines. King Francis I, of France (below) swore by powdered mummy as a tonic! In the nineteenth century, mummy parts were used as ornaments, and mummy unwrappings were social events. Modern cryogenics allows people to be "frozen" scientifically when they die, in the hope that they can be revived in the future.

Still more to discover?

Despite centuries of exploration and discovery, there are still a great number of mysteries to be solved. Many sites still need to be excavated. Only recently the remains of Khufu's Valley Temple and an ancient bakery were unearthed, and in 1995 an amazing discovery was made in the Valley of the Kings – the rock-cut tombs of several sons of Ramses II. Every year, there are new ideas and theories about how and why the pyramids were built. UPUAUT II has shown that there are still many undiscovered secrets. How much more is there to find? Will our ideas be proved correct? Whatever happens, the my pyramids will continue to intrigue people worldwide for centuries to come.

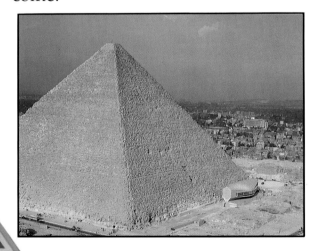

TIME

c. 5000-3100 B.C. **Predynastic Period**
Upper & Lower Egypt formed

c. 3100-2686 B.C. **Archaic Period**
(Dynasties I-II)
Upper & Lower Egypt united

c. 2686-2150 B.C. **Old Kingdom**
(Dynasties III-VI)

c. 2686-2649 Zoser
c. 2680 Step Pyramid built
c. 2589-2566 Khufu
c. 2580 Great Pyramid built
c. 2666-2505 Khafre & Menkure

c. 2150-2040 B.C. **First Intermediate Period**
(Dynasties VII-X)
Collapse of rule of the Kings

c. 2040-1640 B.C. **Middle Kingdom**
(Dynasties XI-XIII)
c. 2040 Egypt reunited

c. 1640-1552 B.C. **Second Intermediate Period (Dynasties XIV-XVII)**
Invasion by foreigners called Hyksos; they are later driven out

c. 1552-1085 B.C. **New Kingdom (Dynasties XVIII-XX)**
Kings buried in Valley of the Kings

c. 1085-664 B.C. **Third Intermediate
Period (Dynasties XXI-XXV)**

c. 664-332 B.C. **Late Period
(Dynasties XXVI-XXX)**
c. 525-404 & 341-332 Persians take Egypt

605-562 **B.C.** *City of Babylon rebuilt*

LINE

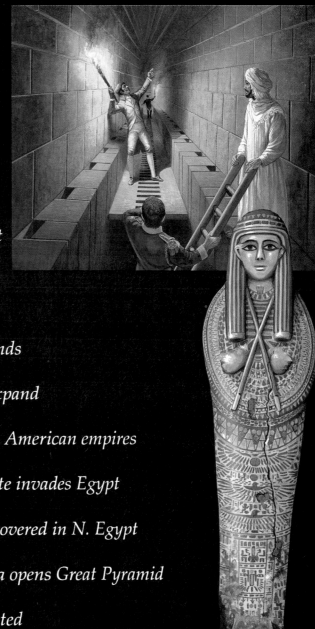

332 B.C. *Alexander the Great conquers Egypt*

323-30 B.C. *The Ptolemies rule Egypt*

30 B.C. *Egypt becomes part of Roman Empire*

A.D. 639-642 *Arab forces invade and rule Egypt*

A.D. 700-1200 *North American mound cities built*

A.D. 950-1200 *Toltecs invade and rule Maya lands*

1400s *Aztec and Inca empires expand*

1500s *Spanish take South American empires*

1798 *Napoléon Bonaparte invades Egypt*

1799 *Rosetta Stone discovered in N. Egypt*

1817 *Giovanni Caviglia opens Great Pyramid*

1822 *Hieroglyphs translated*

1850 *Auguste Mariette excavates Saqqara*

1900-now *Excavations at Saqqara & Giza*

1922 *Tomb of Tutankhamen discovered*

1994 *UPUAUT II finds tiny door in Queen's chamber shaft of Great Pyramid at Giza*

1995 *Rock-cut tombs of several sons of Ramses II discovered in Valley of the Kings*

1996 *Scientists investigate the possibility that Tutankhamen was murdered*

VENUS
Rocky; liquid core
Diameter: 7,521 miles
Distance from Sun: 67 million miles
Number of moons: 0

MARS
Rocky ball; iron-rich core
Diameter: 4,220 miles
Distance from Sun: 142 million miles
Number of moons: 2

MERCURY
Ball of rock; iron-rich core
Diameter: 3,030 miles
Distance from Sun: 36 million miles
Number of moons: 0

EARTH
Rocky ball; metallic core
Diameter: 7,926 miles
Distance from Sun: 93 million miles
Number of moons: 1

JUPITER *(right)*
Gas and liquid gases; small rocky core
Diameter: 88,700 miles
Distance from Sun: 483 million miles
Number of moons: 16

SATURN
Gas and liquid gases; small rocky core
Diameter: 75,000 miles
Distance from Sun: 936 million miles
Number of moons: 18

NEPTUNE
Ball of gas; metal core
Diameter: 30,800 miles
Distance from Sun: 2,794 million miles
Number of moons: 8

PLUTO
Ball of rock and ice
Diameter: 1,800 miles
Distance from Sun: 3,660 million miles
Number of moons: 1

URANUS
Gas; rocky core
Diameter: 32,300 miles
Distance from Sun: 1,783 million miles
Number of moons: 15

Chapter Two
THE UNIVERSE

"*Ever since the dawn of civilization, people have not been content to see events as unconnected and inexplicable... today we still yearn to know why we are here and where we came from. And our goal is nothing less than a complete description of the universe we live in.*"
Stephen Hawking,
A Brief History of Time

Introduction to THE UNIVERSE

The mysteries of the night sky have fascinated scientists, writers, artists, and many other people throughout history. Every civilization has tried to understand our universe, but although many great discoveries have been made, we are still a long way from knowing all its secrets. The twentieth century saw many enormous breakthroughs in the exploration of space, and new, more complex technology is constantly being created to help us fulfill our quest for knowledge.

Our universe is teeming with satellites, probes, and telescopes, all with one purpose – to unravel the tangled secrets of space. How, and when did the universe begin? Will we ever find life in other galaxies? Could black holes make time travel possible? Is there a tenth planet (Planet X) in our solar system? Will our universe get bigger and bigger until it eventually freezes, or will it shrink and collapse in a big crunch?

Perhaps one day we will know the answers to all these questions, and to the thousands more that have perplexed people for hundreds of years. For the moment, we can only try to reach deeper and deeper into the mysteries of our universe.

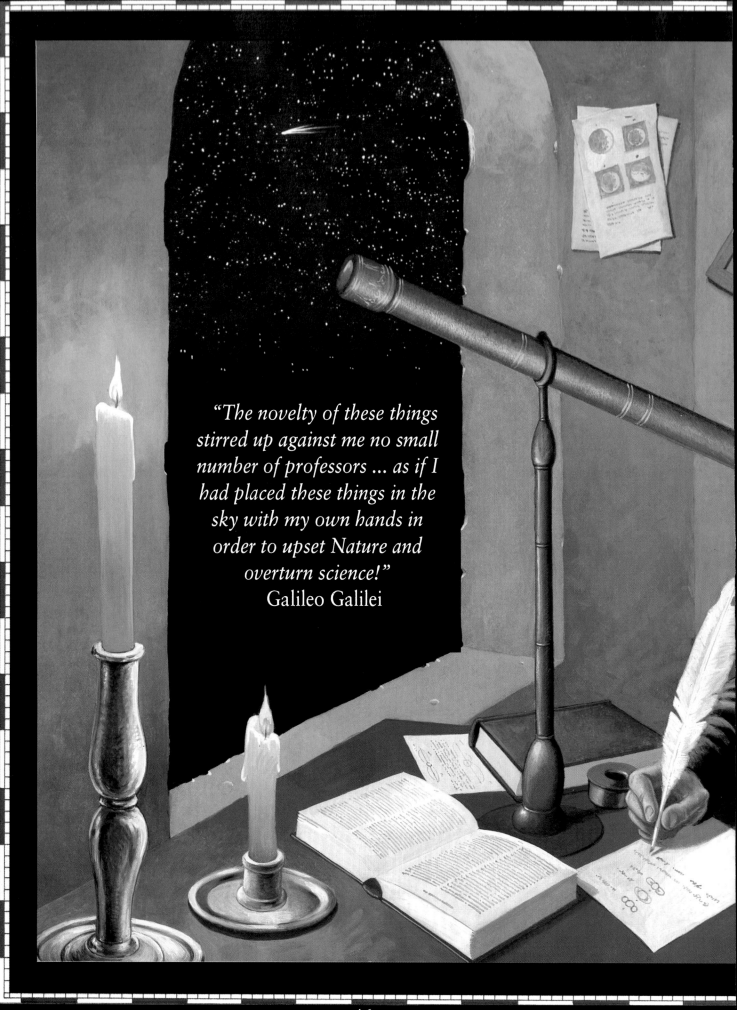

"*The novelty of these things stirred up against me no small number of professors ... as if I had placed these things in the sky with my own hands in order to upset Nature and overturn science!*"
Galileo Galilei

The Mysterious UNIVERSE

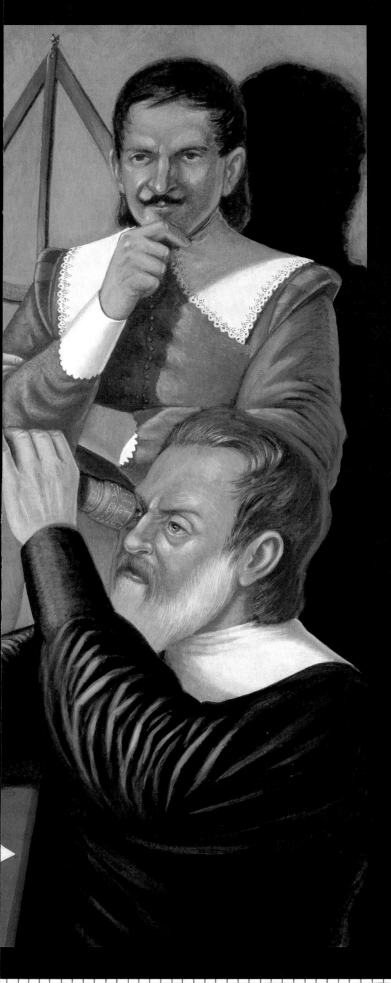

Galileo Galilei (1564–1642) was the first astronomer to look at the sky through a telescope. What he saw when he turned toward the planet Jupiter, on January 7, 1610, astonished him. "Four tiny little stars" were seen in close orbit. They were Jupiter's moons. Their discovery was a challenge to the Christian Church's belief that the Earth was the center of the universe. They proved that not everything moved around the Earth.

Other people before Galileo had the same idea, including the Polish priest Nicolaus Copernicus (1473–1543), but Galileo now had solid evidence. The Catholic Pope said the idea was "false and absurd." Galileo retired, but in 1632 published his support for Copernicus's ideas. He was summoned to the Pope and threatened with torture. He finally rejected his theory, but he muttered, "E pur si muove" ("And yet it does move"). He stayed under house arrest, unable to leave his home, until his death in 1642.

The First MYSTERIES

Since the dawn of civilization, people have been fascinated by the mysteries of the heavens. The ancient Babylonians and Greeks were the first to divide the stars in the sky into groups called *constellations*, which are still used today. They also watched the movements of the planets, and recorded the arrival of comets and the behavior of supernovae (exploding stars). The Egyptian pyramids and the stone circle of Stonehenge, in England, are thought to have been inspired by astronomical events. But these people had no idea what the universe was made of, nor of its vast size. They thought of the Earth as flat, below a canopy of stars which revolved around the planet once a day.

SUN WORSHIP
As discussed on page 26, the ancient Egyptians believed that the sky was the goddess Nut (left) and that the Sun was the god Re (or Ra). When members of the royal family died, boats were often put in their tombs so that they could join Re on his heavenly journey.

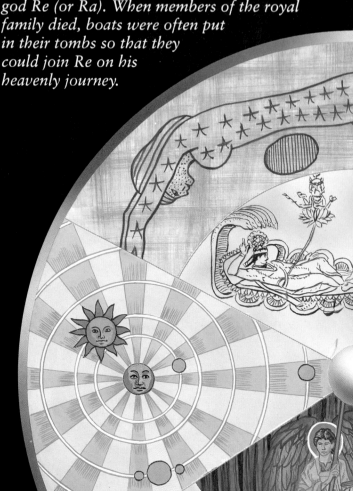

THE PLACE OF THE EARTH
Most ancient Greeks believed that the Earth lay at the center of the universe. Ptolemy (A.D. 100–165), a great Greek astronomer, argued that the stars and planets must move around the Earth in circles, because the circle was a perfect shape created by the gods. His description of how the universe worked was accepted for more than 1,500 years.

ANCIENT DISCOVERIES
The Greek scholar Aristotle (384–322 B.C.) proved that the Earth must be round. He explained that when the Earth's shadow passes in front of the Moon during eclipses (see page 57), its edge appears to be curved, so it must be spherical in shape.

THE HEAVENLY SUN

The Sun has been worshiped as a god for thousands of years, by many different peoples. Ancient Hindus called the Sun-god Surya. He was one of the three main gods in their Holy Book of Divine Knowledge. In the fifth century B.C., ancient Greek religion linked the Sun to the god Apollo.

How many stars are there? With the naked eye, we can see about 2,000 stars on a clear night. But our galaxy alone contains 100,000 million stars. The entire universe probably contains at least a billion trillion stars – 1,000,000,000,000,000,000,000,000 of them!

LIGHTS IN THE SKY

Strange happenings in the skies caused fear and panic in ancient times, as they were believed to be omens of disaster. Comets frightened many people, while aurorae, or natural displays of brightly colored lights, were believed to be angry gods.

Foretelling the future

Astrology is based on the ancient belief that the stars and planets control our lives. The signs of the zodiac represent the twelve constellations of stars through which the Sun appears to pass every year. An astrologer casts a horoscope from a person's date and place of birth. This predicts that person's future, based on the constellations.

THE CURVED EARTH

The Earth appeared flat, but Aristotle realized it was not. He knew that the number of stars you can see in the sky depends on where you are. The bright star Canopus can be seen from Egypt, but not from Greece. This would not happen if the Earth were flat.

HEAVENLY BLISS

The sky used to be seen as a solid canopy, not much higher than the highest mountains, with the stars set into it like jewels. Many religions believe that the heavens contain a better world to which good people go after they die, while those who have been bad in their lifetime are doomed to live underground.

Changing Views of THE UNIVERSE

The first challenge to Ptolemy's Earth-centered universe came from Nicolaus Copernicus, in 1543. He realized that the movement of the planets was explained more easily if the Sun, not the Earth, lay at the center. But he did not dare publish his theories until the year of his death. Like Ptolemy, he believed that the planets moved in circles, but Johannes Kepler (1571-1630) showed that their orbits were elliptical (oval-shaped). To explain this, Isaac Newton (1643-1727) discovered the laws of gravity (the force which attracts objects toward each other). In the twentieth century, Albert Einstein's theories linked gravity, space, and time to explain the shape of the universe.

How big is the universe?
The universe is so big that light, which travels at 186,000 miles (300,000 km) per second, would take billions of years to reach us from its furthest edges.

REDRAWING THE UNIVERSE
Copernicus did not support Ptolemy's idea that all the stars circled the Earth once a day. He also realized that it could not explain all the movements of the Sun, Moon, and planets. His own theory declared the Earth an ordinary planet instead of the center of the universe.

THE PULL OF THE EARTH
Isaac Newton's theory of gravity applies equally to an apple falling from a tree and to the movement of the planets. He said that all objects are pulled together by a force based on their mass (the matter they contain) and their distance apart. This is why planets' orbits are elliptical.

EARLY OBSERVATIONS

Galileo used his telescope to confirm that Copernicus had been right to put the Sun at the center of the universe. The telescope was invented in 1608 by a Dutch eyeglass-maker, Hans Lippershey, who called it a "looker." He found that two lenses in a tube could magnify distant objects. When Galileo heard of this, he quickly built his own telescope, which he used to make many amazing discoveries.

SEEING INTO SPACE

Tycho Brahe (1546–1601) was a Danish astronomer who built an observatory and kept precise records of the stars and planets. His assistant, Johannes Kepler (1571–1630), later used these records to show that the planets moved in elliptical (oval-shaped) orbits, rather than in circles.

A MODERN GENIUS

Albert Einstein (1879–1955) was one of the greatest physicists of the twentieth century. His theory combines space and time so that objects are given a position in time as well as in space. Gravity works by bending this space-time, making objects follow a curved path.

Fact or fiction?

Some of the most fantastic predictions of science fiction have come true. But so far we have not met aliens, or discovered a "warp drive" to travel at the speed of light. If Einstein was right, such speeds are impossible, so most of the universe will always be out of our reach.

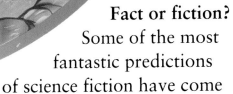

"As long as the Moon shall rise,
As long as the rivers shall flow,
As long as the Sun shall shine,
As long as the grass shall grow."
Native American rhyme for treaties that
are meant to last forever.

The Solar SYSTEM

One star, nine planets, and a collection of asteroids, comets, and moons make up our solar system, the only part of the universe within range of modern spacecraft. Only the Earth has all the right conditions to have evolved into the planet we know. At the center of the solar system is the Sun, the star around which all the nine planets rotate. The planets lie in a flat, disklike shape, suggesting that they were formed from a disk of dust and gas spinning around the Sun. Most of the planets have their own moons: Earth and Pluto have one, Mars has two, Neptune eight, Uranus 15, Jupiter 16, and Saturn 18. Between the orbits of Mars and Jupiter there are more than 3,500 asteroids, or chunks of rock, ranging from 600 miles to less than 1 mile in diameter. There may be thousands of even smaller asteroids, which are too tiny to be seen from Earth. There may also be a tenth planet (Planet X) hidden beyond Pluto.

The Sun and its PLANETS

The Sun is the center and energy source of the solar system. It is over a million times the size of the Earth but only 330,000 times its mass, and consists mainly of the gases hydrogen and helium. Its energy comes from the hydrogen atoms joining together. At the Sun's surface, the temperature is 11,030°F, but in the center it is even hotter, at 30 million °F. The Earth orbits the Sun once a year, at a distance of about 93 million miles. In a spacecraft traveling at the top speed of a normal car, it would take 100 years to get from the Earth to the Sun!

**WARNING:
NEVER LOOK DIRECTLY
AT THE SUN**

Will the Sun ever run out of fuel?
Yes, but not for awhile. Every second, 600 million tons of hydrogen are changed into helium in the Sun. In about five billion years, the hydrogen will run out, the Sun will stop radiating energy, and all life on Earth will die.

Turn to page 42 for more facts about the planets.

THE POWERHOUSE OF THE SOLAR SYSTEM
Every second, the Sun converts four million tons of its gases into energy. At its surface, bursts of gas and energy leap out, called flares *and* prominences. *These produce so much energy that they can be felt on Earth as magnetic storms.*

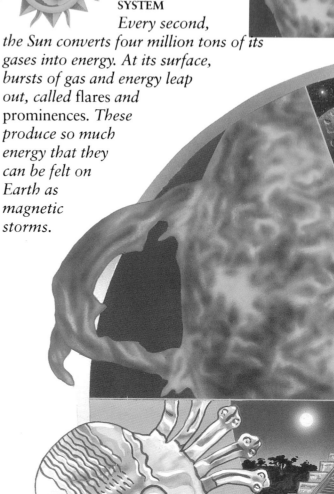

THE DIVINE SUN
The Aztecs of Mexico and Central America believed that their world began when the gods sacrificed themselves to create the Sun. To help the Sun in its nightly battles with the Moon and stars, the Aztecs built huge temples, where they offered sacrifices and prayers.

THE INNER PLANETS

The four planets which are nearest to the Sun are Mercury, Venus, Earth, and Mars. These are made of rock and metal. They are often called the terrestrial planets because they are similar to the Earth.

Mercury

Venus

Earth

Mars

Mercury is small, bare, and so close to the Sun that its surface can reach temperatures up to 884°F. Venus is the planet nearest in size to the Earth, but it is very hot and is surrounded by clouds of sulfuric acid. Mars is covered with red rocks and dust, but is one of the few planets to have an atmosphere and frozen poles, like our North and South Poles.

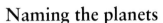

Naming the planets

The ancient Romans and Greeks knew only five planets – apart from the Earth – and gave them the names of their gods. Mercury was the Roman god of trade, Venus the goddess of love, and Mars the god of war. Jupiter controlled the weather, and Saturn was the father of the gods. The outer planets, discovered later, were also named after gods.

Uranus   **Saturn**   **Jupiter**

Neptune

Pluto

THE OUTER PLANETS

Jupiter, Saturn, Uranus, and Neptune are huge, fast-spinning planets, which are made up mostly of gas and some liquid. They are so gaseous that no spacecraft can land on them.

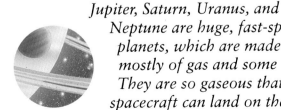

Pluto, however, is small, icy, and solid. Saturn, with its spectacular rings, is the most beautiful planet. The rings are more than 170,000 miles wide, but are only 60–100 feet thick, and consist of dust and chunks of ice orbiting the planet. Saturn is so light that it would float on water!

The Mysterious MOONS

The Moon, our nearest neighbor and the only object in space to which people have traveled, is just over 238,000 miles away – no distance at all in space! The Moon's cold light, its changing shape, and the markings on its surface have made it a fascinating object since the earliest times. Many ancient civilizations worshiped the Moon as a god. No other inner planet has a moon quite like ours: Mercury and Venus have no moons at all, and the two moons of Mars are tiny. The outer planets have so many moons that some remain to be discovered, but only four identified moons are bigger than our own.

The changing Moon
The Moon does not shine, but reflects sunlight. The changes of the Moon (phases) are due to the angles of the Earth, Sun, and Moon. With a new Moon, the side lit by the Sun faces away from the Earth. The Moon orbits, and more of the side facing the Earth is lit, until the Moon looks full.

"The Eagle has landed"
On July 20, 1969, humans set foot on the Moon for the first time. The U.S. Apollo 11 spacecraft took Neil Armstrong, "Buzz" Aldrin, and Michael Collins to a landing in the Sea of Tranquility, and brought them safely home. By 1972, another ten people had visited the Moon, but nobody has been back since. The Apollo missions found that the Moon was a bare, cratered land, with rocks very much like those on Earth.

THE FACE OF OUR MOON

The Moon revolves in exactly the same time it takes to orbit the Earth, so it always shows us the same face. Its surface is pitted with craters caused by rocks crashing into it. Volcanoes have also shaped its surface, by pouring out molten lava to form pits or "seas" which never contained water. Throughout history, many peoples have thought they could see figures like rabbits within the Moon. In ancient Egyptian mythology, the Moon was believed to be the left eye of the god Horus.

CHEESE FEAST
In the Middle Ages, some people believed that the Moon's surface was made of green cheese! We now know that It consists of finely-powdered rock.

Shadows in space

Solar eclipses happen when the Sun, Moon, and Earth lie in a straight line. The Moon seems to block the Sun's light (below). Lunar eclipses occur when the Moon passes through the Earth's shadow. Ancient Chinese people believed that solar eclipses were dragons eating the Sun.

OTHER MOONS
Ganymede, the solar system's largest moon, orbits Jupiter and, at 3,268 miles (5,260 km) in diameter, is 1.5 times bigger than our Moon. Saturn's biggest moon, Titan, is the only moon with a thick atmosphere, which consists of nitrogen, methane, and cyanide. Titan may have oceans of liquid methane.

Where did the Moon come from?
Nobody really knows. The most popular theory is that it was formed when a huge object from space collided with the Earth. The collision hurled up debris from the Earth to form a ring, which became the Moon. Another theory suggests that originally the Moon existed elsewhere in the solar system and was pulled toward the Earth by gravity. However, most scientists think that this is very unlikely.

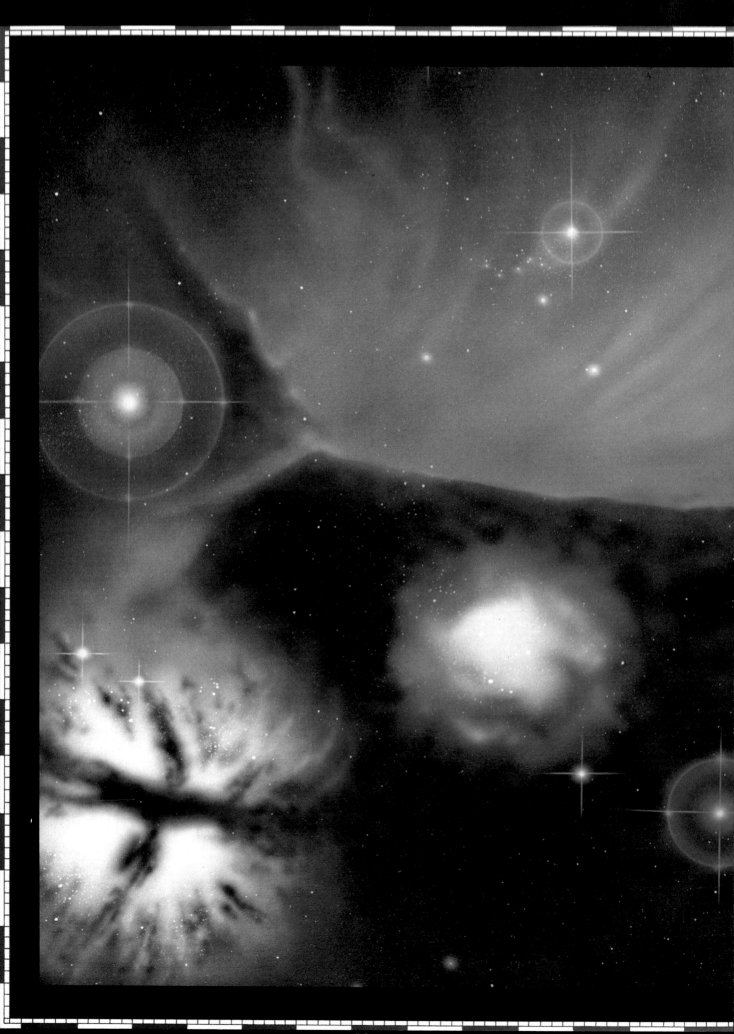

Stars and GALAXIES

The solar system is big, but it is tiny compared to the distances between the stars. They are so far away that even the most powerful telescope on Earth will not show them as more than points of light. The stars are not spread evenly throughout space, but are grouped into large clusters, or galaxies. Our own galaxy, the Milky Way, contains 100,000 million stars. Traveling at the speed of light, it would take more than four years to get to the nearest one, Proxima Centauri. At that speed we would reach our own star, the Sun, in just eight minutes. To get to Andromeda, the nearest galaxy outside the Milky Way, it would take 2.2 million years.

Stars vary in brightness, depending on how bright and how far away they are. The brightest, which can be seen with the naked eye, have their own names, and ancient people grouped them into constellations. The stars in a constellation appear close together, but this is not true – some are further away from the Earth than others.

"Awake! for Morning in the Bowl of Night
Has flung the Stone that turns the Stars to flight
And lo! The Hunter of the East has caught
The Sultan's Turret in a Noose of Light."
Omar Khayyam, Persian poet and astronomer (1048–1131), translated by Edward Fitzgerald

Comets and SHOOTING STARS

Comets were once believed to be stars. They used to strike fear into human beings, because their arrival was thought to announce some great event, such as the death of a ruler. We now know that comets are icy wanderers from the edges of the solar system, which swing close to the Sun every so often. They become visible as they are heated by the Sun, turning the ice into vapor which forms a tail. When the Earth passes through the dust left by a comet, the particles burn up in the atmosphere as meteors.

WHAT ARE COMETS?

Comets are dirty snowballs, ranging from the size of a house to a few miles across. They are made of soot, dust, and ice, and are much too small to see until they approach the Sun. As they get closer, the heat of the Sun turns the ice into steam, or vapor. This makes a glowing cloud and a long, glowing tail which always points away from the Sun and streams behind the comet as it journeys across the sky. At this stage it is possible to see the comet from the Earth. Scientists think that there might be millions of comets traveling through space.

A regular visitor

The most famous comet of all is Halley's Comet, which reappears every 76 years. It was named by the eighteenth-century astronomer Edmund Halley. In 1986, the comet was examined by the Giotto spacecraft, and was found to be shaped like a potato, 9 miles (15 km) long and 5 miles (8.3 km) across.

COMETS IN HISTORY

Comet sightings have been recorded since ancient times. It may have been a comet, not a star, that appeared at the birth of Christ, as told in the Bible. The medieval Bayeux Tapestry in France shows people marveling at Halley's Comet, which made one of its appearances in 1066.

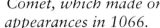

How many shooting stars are there? Every day, 300 tons of dust and rock fall into the Earth's atmosphere. Almost all of this consists of tiny particles that burn up, forming meteors. Millions of particles hit the planet every day, but most of them are so tiny that an observer on Earth will see only about 10 shooting stars per hour.

DRAGONS IN THE SKY

Meteorites are chunks of rock from the asteroids in the solar system. They are too big to burn up when they enter the Earth's atmosphere, and hit the ground. They are clearly visible in the sky, and can be terrifying. Meteorites have frightened people throughout history. They were often believed to be huge, fiery dragons coming to attack the world, or weapons of revenge sent by the angry gods to destroy the Earth.

COLLISION

In July 1994, the comet Shoemaker-Levy 9 collided with the planet Jupiter. It was broken into more than 20 pieces before impact, but it still left huge craters.

CRASH!

When a huge meteorite landed near Tunguska, Siberia, in 1908 (below), it destroyed the surrounding forests for miles, leaving the landscape desolate and ruined. Luckily, nobody was hurt.

ARE WE IN DANGER?

About 50,000 years ago, a large meteorite hit Arizona, making a vast crater. If a really huge meteorite hit Earth, its effect might be deadly.

The Starry SKIES

Like human beings, stars are born, grow old, and die. If we look hard enough, we can find stars of every age in the sky. Stars are formed from clouds of hydrogen gas collapsing under the force of gravity and turning into helium gas, in a process that produces huge amounts of energy. Near the end of the lives of giant stars, the helium changes into even heavier substances. Eventually these giant stars blow up in huge explosions called supernovae, scattering elements like carbon, silicon, iron, and oxygen into space. New stars and planets form from this debris. The Earth and everything in it, including ourselves, is in fact made of recycled material from a long-dead star.

Into the void

After a huge star explodes, the core is left behind and collapses into a tiny point – a black hole. The pull of gravity from a black hole is so strong that not even light can escape from it.

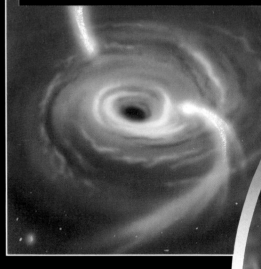

THE LIFE OF A STAR

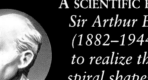

A star like the Sun begins as a cloud of gas and dust, which is gradually squashed by the force of gravity to make the star. At the end of its life it swells up into a "red giant" star, then puffs off its outer layers of gas into space. Even our Sun will finally end its life as a tiny "white dwarf" star.

GIANTS AND DWARFS

The biggest stars, or "red giants," have a lot of pressure in their core, burn quickly and brightly and die earliest, leaving the core as a "white dwarf." Tiny, dim stars, or "brown dwarfs," never become true stars. They get gradually fainter, and finally fade into "black dwarfs."

A SCIENTIFIC BREAKTHROUGH

Sir Arthur Eddington (1882–1944) was the first person to realize that the mysterious spiral shapes seen in the sky were galaxies. He also proved that Einstein's theory of gravity was correct, by watching light being bent during an eclipse in 1919. Eddington wrote several famous books that explained the nature of the universe in a simple, understandable way.

OUR OWN GALAXY

The Milky Way is a spiral-shaped galaxy. Our solar system is on one of the "arms" of the galaxy, about two-thirds of the way out.

STAR PULSES

Super-dense stars called neutron stars, which measure about 20 miles across, spin quickly and send out radio signals. The regular pulses picked up from these stars by large radio receivers on Earth give them the name pulsars.

PATTERNS IN SPACE

Galaxies form in four different shapes. Spiral galaxies are like pinwheels, and the oldest stars are contained in elliptical (oval-shaped) galaxies. Barred spiral galaxies have a thick line running through the middle. Other galaxies have irregular shapes, depending on the number of stars and their position in space.

What would happen if I fell feet first into a black hole?
You would be stretched out like a piece of spaghetti, because the force at your feet would be stronger than that at your head. Then you would disappear beyond the "event horizon." Nothing, not even light, can escape from the black hole once it has passed this point.

THE BRIGHTEST STAR

Eta Carinae is the most luminous known star of all. It is 150 times bigger than the Sun, and six million times brighter.

THE CONSTELLATIONS

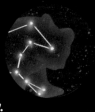

There are 88 identified constellations in the universe. Each has its own area of the sky, decided in 1930. The constellations are useful for finding your way around the sky.

Exploring the
UNIVERSE

Our knowledge of the universe depends on observation – through telescopes, radio telescopes, and satellites. The universe is so vast that we can never hope to travel far beyond the edges of the solar system. But many amazing things can be discovered simply by looking at our universe. We can tell what stars are made of, how far away they are, how fast they are moving, and how hot, bright, or old they are. By putting telescopes on the tops of mountains, we can see much further and much more clearly than at ground level, because there is less air and pollution to look through, and therefore the image is clearer. Telescopes in space, such as the Hubble telescope, work even better, and produce incredibly clear pictures. Nearly 400 years of observation through telescopes have shown that the universe is indeed mysterious, and that there must be many strange things waiting to be discovered.

"My own suspicion is that the universe is not only queerer than we suppose, but queerer than we can suppose."
J.B.S. Haldane

Observing the UNIVERSE

Bigger telescopes work better than smaller ones, because they collect more light and can detect dimmer and more distant objects. However, if lenses are too big they can be so heavy that they bend, making the image less accurate. Curved mirrors work better because they reflect the light and therefore can be supported from behind. Electronic devices can be used to collect and record results more accurately than the human eye. But even the most powerful telescopes on Earth cannot show all the details of a distant star or the planets orbiting it.

THE FIRST TELESCOPES

Galileo's telescope, built in 1609, consisted of two lenses mounted at either end of a tube. By 1671, Isaac Newton had invented a reflecting telescope that used mirrors. In 1845, the Earl of Rosse built a 72-inch (180-cm) reflecting telescope, with which he discovered the spiral shape of some galaxies. In 1931, Karl Jansky accidentally discovered radio waves coming from the Milky Way. These inspired Grote Reber to invent the first radio telescope in 1936, which allowed astronomers to explore the universe in greater detail.

OBSERVATORIES

Highly polluted cities such as Los Angeles and London are too dirty for a good, clear view of the stars. Therefore, more remote spots have been found. The best modern observatories are on mountains in Hawaii and the Canary Islands, and similar areas with clear, clean skies.

The U.S. Orbiting Solar Observatory satellites are the primary astronomical observatories in space. The first was launched in 1962.

A pioneering vision

The Hubble space telescope, launched in 1990, has a 94-inch (235-cm) reflector and orbits 370 miles (618 km) above the Earth. The mirror was made in the wrong shape, but in 1993 it was repaired in space. Hubble is sending back the clearest pictures of distant objects ever taken.

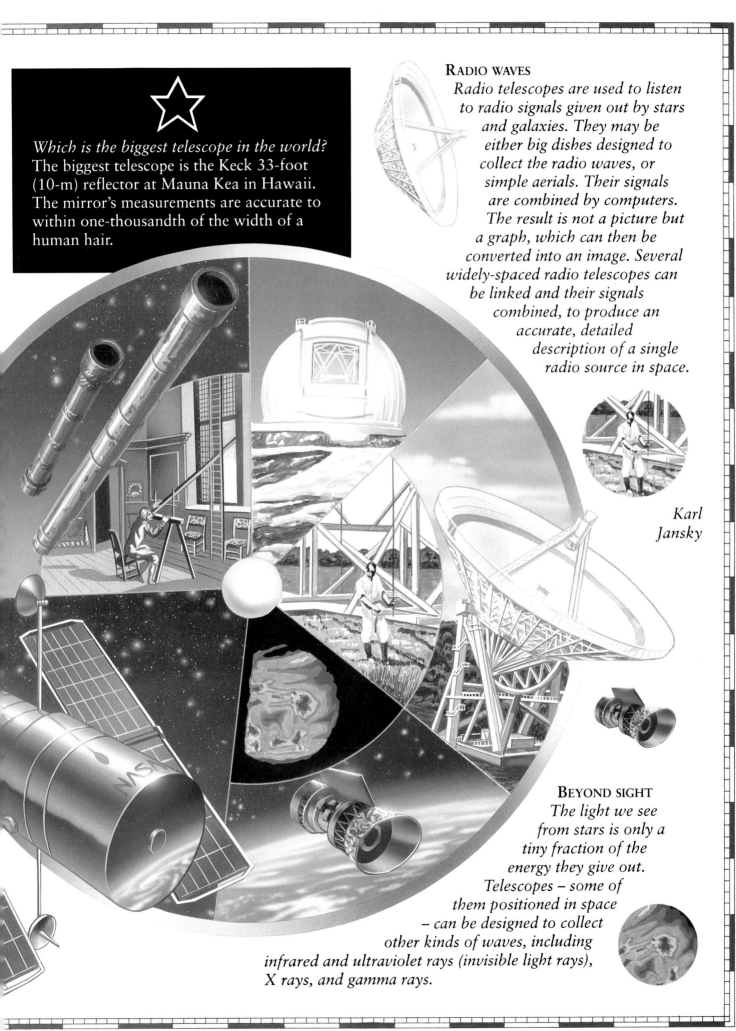

Which is the biggest telescope in the world?
The biggest telescope is the Keck 33-foot
(10-m) reflector at Mauna Kea in Hawaii.
The mirror's measurements are accurate to
within one-thousandth of the width of a
human hair.

RADIO WAVES

Radio telescopes are used to listen
to radio signals given out by stars
and galaxies. They may be
either big dishes designed to
collect the radio waves, or
simple aerials. Their signals
are combined by computers.
The result is not a picture but
a graph, which can then be
converted into an image. Several
widely-spaced radio telescopes can
be linked and their signals
combined, to produce an
accurate, detailed
description of a single
radio source in space.

Karl
Jansky

BEYOND SIGHT

The light we see
from stars is only a
tiny fraction of the
energy they give out.
Telescopes – some of
them positioned in space
– can be designed to collect
other kinds of waves, including
infrared and ultraviolet rays (invisible light rays),
X rays, and gamma rays.

Fantastic VOYAGES

With the development of the rocket, people's dreams of space travel finally came true. Rockets burn fuel to produce gases that escape through a nozzle, causing the rocket to thrust forward. Their engines are the only kind that can work in space, and they must carry all their fuel and oxygen to burn it. The secret of reaching space is the multi-stage rocket, in which various parts burn out and fall off, one after another. Since the first rockets went into space, spacecraft have explored the solar system to its very limits, and people have walked on the Moon.

A VISION OF THE FUTURE
The French author Jules Verne was well known for his futuristic visions. In 1865 he wrote a book about a journey to the Moon. His space travelers were fired from a gun – which in real life would have killed them – and had to fly around the Moon, and then come back, because they had no way of landing.

THE ROCKET PIONEERS
The principles of rocketry were developed by Konstantin Tsiolkovsky, a Russian teacher, at the beginning of the twentieth century. Robert Goddard, an American physicist whose early rocket is shown bottom left, and Werner von Braun (above) from Germany went on to build and launch successful rockets. Von Braun's V-2 rocket (top left) was used by the Nazis as a devastating weapon during the last year of World War II (1939–1945).

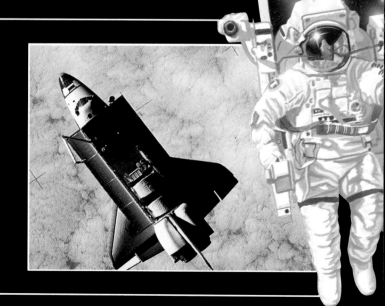

NASA
The National Aeronautics and Space Administration (NASA) put the first person on the Moon in July 1969. But unstaffed NASA missions to the planets have taught us more. For example, the landings on Mars by Viking spacecraft found no signs of life there, despite many people's claims that it could exist.

Can we make time stand still?
If we can ever design a spacecraft that is able to travel at the speed of light, time on board will stand still, according to Albert Einstein's theories. An astronaut could travel for 1,000 years and come back no older than the day he or she set off. But it is unlikely that technology will ever develop enough to build such a fast craft.

ALONE IN SPACE
The first person in space, Major Yuri Gagarin, was launched by the former Soviet Union in Vostok 1 on April 12, 1961. He completed a single orbit of the Earth, and landed safely.

PROBING DEEP SPACE
The first space probes to leave the solar system were Pioneer 10 and 11, then two Voyager spacecraft. The Voyager craft took closeup pictures of Jupiter and Saturn in 1979, then Voyager 2 went on to visit Uranus and Neptune. The latest mission, Galileo, was launched in 1989 but will reach the outer planets slowly, by a complicated route.

LITTER-BUGS
The landscapes of the solar system are dotted with equipment left behind by various expeditions.

EARTH'S CALLING CARD
Pioneer 10, which was launched in 1972, carries a plaque of information, or "calling card," in case it should ever meet other intelligent life. It has a diagram showing what human beings look like, and a sky map to identify where our solar system is.

The Future of the UNIVERSE

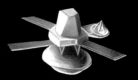

> "We find ourselves in a bewildering world. We want to make sense of what we see around us and to ask: What is the nature of the universe? What is our place in it and where did it and we come from? Why is it the way it is?"
> Stephen Hawking,
> *A Brief History of Time*

Nearly all astronomers believe that the universe began with a big bang. About 15 billion years ago, the universe was incredibly hot and very small – even smaller than an atom. Then it began to expand at a very fast rate. Today, everything in the universe is still moving apart. Various recent discoveries have provided strong evidence that this theory is correct.

If the universe began with a big bang, how will it end? That is much more uncertain. It may go on expanding forever, or it may stop expanding, start shrinking, and eventually end in a big crunch sometime in the distant future. It all depends on how much material the universe contains. If there is enough material, the pull of its gravity will be strong enough to stop the universe from expanding and eventually make it collapse in a big crunch. Of course, this wouldn't happen for millions of years!

Is There Anybody OUT THERE?

Are we alone in our universe? If life evolved (developed) naturally on Earth, as most scientists believe, it has probably evolved somewhere else too. There are so many billions of stars similar to the Sun that many of them must have planets. Among those planets there might be some with conditions like those on Earth. If so, then we are almost certainly not alone. To find other intelligent life, we must constantly listen and observe. For more than 30 years, radio telescopes have been pointed at the stars to try to pick up any radio signals from distant civilizations – but so far without success. The search for life in our universe goes on, and may continue forever.

HAVE WE MET BEFORE?
Mysterious lines are clearly visible across the desert in Peru, and are thought by some people to be the work of ancient aliens.

A LONG HISTORY
Throughout history, strange, unknown lights in the sky have made people wonder about other life in the universe.

LIFE ON MARS?
The astronomer Percival Lowell (1855–1916) believed that he could see canals on Mars, evidence of intelligent life there. But these were optical illusions, as photographs by the Viking spacecraft proved.

Is there proof of life in other galaxies?
In 1995, British ufologists (people who study UFOs) claimed that they had seen a U.S. government film from 1947. They claimed it showed scientists examining the body of an alien whose craft crashed in New Mexico. Could this solve one of the greatest mysteries of our universe?

LIGHTS IN THE SKY
Many people have seen strange, disk-shaped objects in the sky. These have been named Unidentified Flying Objects, *or UFOs. But in spite of many rumors and continuous observation of the skies, there is no hard evidence that they are alien spacecraft. Most UFOs are probably oddly-shaped clouds, or have been cleverly faked in photographs.*

THE FACE OF MARS

Lowell's theories of Martian life were proved wrong, but years later, a picture taken by a Viking probe seemed to show a face carved on the planet's surface.

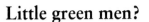

Was this evidence of an ancient Martian civilization? Unfortunately not. The human eye is so good at recognizing faces that it can easily trick the brain into thinking it can see one – in a rock of roughly the right shape or a landscape covered with shadows, for example.

Little green men?

Most images of aliens have been created in films such as *E.T.* Aliens are often shown as green or gray in color, have large eyes, and talk slowly and carefully. A real alien would probably be quite different, and might think that we look really weird. Or it might look exactly the same as a human!

A NATIONAL ALERT

The War of the Worlds, *by the English writer H.G. Wells, describes an invasion of the Earth by Martians.*

The novel was written in England in 1898, and was turned into a radio play in 1938. When it was broadcast, the story was so convincing that thousands of listeners thought it was a real news bulletin, and ran screaming into the streets in their pajamas. Many other futuristic novels have since been written, but none had such a dramatic effect!

The Unsolved MYSTERIES

The greatest unsolved mystery of the universe is how much of it there is. Spiral galaxies keep their shape so well that they must contain far more material than we can see. In fact, visible stars make up probably only about one-tenth of the total mass (material) of the universe. So what makes up the rest, or the "missing mass?" It might be stars that are too dim to see, but in fact we just don't know. It is important to find the answer because the mass determines whether the universe will go on expanding forever, ending cold and empty in a big chill, or whether it will eventually shrink into nothingness during a big crunch.

TIME TRAVEL
In films, such as Dr. Who (top) or Back to the Future (left), and books like The Time Machine (right), people travel through time, but will this ever be possible? Einstein's Theory of Relativity suggests that somebody falling into a black hole would not be killed, but might pass through "wormholes" to reach another universe, another part of our universe, or another time.

WORMING THROUGH SPACE
Wormholes are tunnels that link one part of space-time with another. If space-time is curved like the surface of an apple, then a wormhole is like a shortcut to the other side, through which objects might be able to travel from one time to another. It sounds crazy – but it could be true.

The Big Crunch
Many scientists believe that the universe will eventually end as it started – as a single point. If this big crunch does occur, what will happen to the universe next? The whole process might start again with another big bang, to form new stars, planets, and galaxies – and a new Earth?

How many black holes are there? There could be more black holes than the number of visible stars – that is, more than a hundred billion in our galaxy alone. If so, they would account for a lot of the "missing mass" in space, because black holes can contain enough material to make 100,000 suns.

DEADLY IMPACT

Sixty-five million years ago, a huge asteroid hit the Earth, making a cloud of debris that changed the climate, killing the dinosaurs. It could happen again. Astronomers are watching, to give us warning.

PLANET X

Deep in the solar system, there could be a tenth planet. So far, searches for Planet X have failed, but the hunt continues...

COLONIZING MARS

Mars is the only planet close to being able to support life. If it was artificially heated over many centuries, it could perhaps be a new Earth.

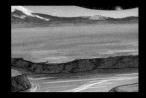

Looking to the future

Our universe was created 15 billion years ago, yet human life has only existed for a tiny fraction of that time. It will take hundreds, perhaps thousands of years for us to come even close to understanding all the secrets of space. With so many new worlds and galaxies to explore and so many questions to answer, it is no wonder that scientists and other people are forever trying to unravel the mysteries of the universe.

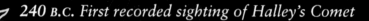

4th century B.C. *Aristotle shows that Earth is round*

240 B.C. *First recorded sighting of Halley's Comet*

2nd century A.D. *Ptolemy creates theory of the universe*

1543 *Copernicus asserts his theory of the solar system*
1572 *Brahe observes stars and planets*

1600 *Kepler shows planets move in elliptical orbits*
1610 *January 7, Galileo sees Jupiter's moons*
1671 *Newton invents reflecting telescope*
1675 *Royal Greenwich Observatory founded*

1807 *Rockets used during Napoleonic War*
1845 *Earl of Rosse builds 72-inch reflecting telescope*
1865 *Verne's* From the Earth to the Moon
1898 *Wells'* The War of the Worlds

1903 *Tsiolkovsky works out basic principles of space flight*

1914 *Eddington identifies spiral galaxies*
1915-1916 *Einstein publishes Theory of Relativity*

1923 *Oberth publishes book on space flight*
1926 *Goddard launches first liquid-propellant rocket*

1930 *Pluto discovered*
1931 *Jansky finds radio waves in space*
1936 *Reber builds radio telescope*

1942 *V-2 rocket reaches height of 150 miles*

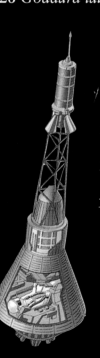

1957 *October 4, Soviet satellite Sputnik 1 launched*
November: Launch of Sputnik 2, with dog Laika
1958 *January 31, U.S. satellite Explorer 1 launched*
July: NASA created
1959 *Soviet Luna 3 probe photographs far side of Moon for first time*
1960 *February: First weather satellite, TIROS 1, launched*
Soviet SS-7 rocket explodes on launchpad, killing many people
First U.S. deep space probe, Pioneer 5, launched
1961 *April 12, Cosmonaut Yuri Gagarin makes single orbit of Earth*
May: Alan Shephard is first American in space
August: Cosmonaut Gherman Titov orbits Earth 16 times

1962 John Glenn is first American to orbit Earth
     April: U.S. probe Ranger 4 strikes Moon
     April 26 British satellite Ariel 1 is launched
     Mariner 2 probe visits Venus
     July: Telstar communications satellite launched
1963 Cosmonaut Valentina Tereshkova is first woman in space
1964 Soviet Union puts 3 people into orbit in Voshkod 1
1965 March: NASA's first staffed Gemini flight
     Alexsei Leonov makes first space walk from Voshkod 2
     July: U.S. probe Mariner 4 photographs Mars
1966 January: Soviet probe Luna 9 lands on Moon
1967 Three Apollo astronauts killed in a launchpad fire
     June: Soviet probe Venera 4 transmits data on Venus
     Pulsars discovered
1968 October: First manned Apollo flight
     December: Three astronauts orbit Moon in Apollo 8
1969 July 20, Apollo 11 lands on Moon

1970 February 11, Osumi, first Japanese satellite, launched
     1971 December: Capsule from Soviet probe, Mars 3, lands on Mars
          November: NASA's probe, Mariner 9, is first to orbit Mars
     1972 Pioneer 10 launched, carrying "calling card"
          1973 May: Skylab 2 launched with crew of three
          1975 July: U.S. Apollo and Soviet Soyuz spacecraft link in space
               October: Soviet probe Venera 9 lands on Venus
               1976 Viking 1 sends photographs from Mars
               1977 August, September: NASA
                    launches Voyagers 1 and 2
                    1979 September: U.S. probe
                    Pioneer-Saturn flies past Saturn
                    and transmits data to Earth

               1981 April: First flight of U.S.
               space shuttle Columbia
               1983 U.S. announces Strategic
               Defense initiative ("Star Wars")

     June: Pioneer 10 travels beyond all planets
          November: Spacelab, built by European Space
          Agency (ESA), launched
     1986 January: Challenger space shuttle explodes
          February: Launch of Mir space station
          March: Giotto photographs Halley's Comet
          1988 U.S. space program resumed with
          launch of shuttle Discovery
          November: launch of Buran shuttle

     1990 Hubble space telescope launched
1992 Shuttle astronauts make eight-hour space walk
Cosmic Background Explorer satellite discovers echo of Big Bang
1994 July: Comet Shoemaker-Levy collides with Jupiter

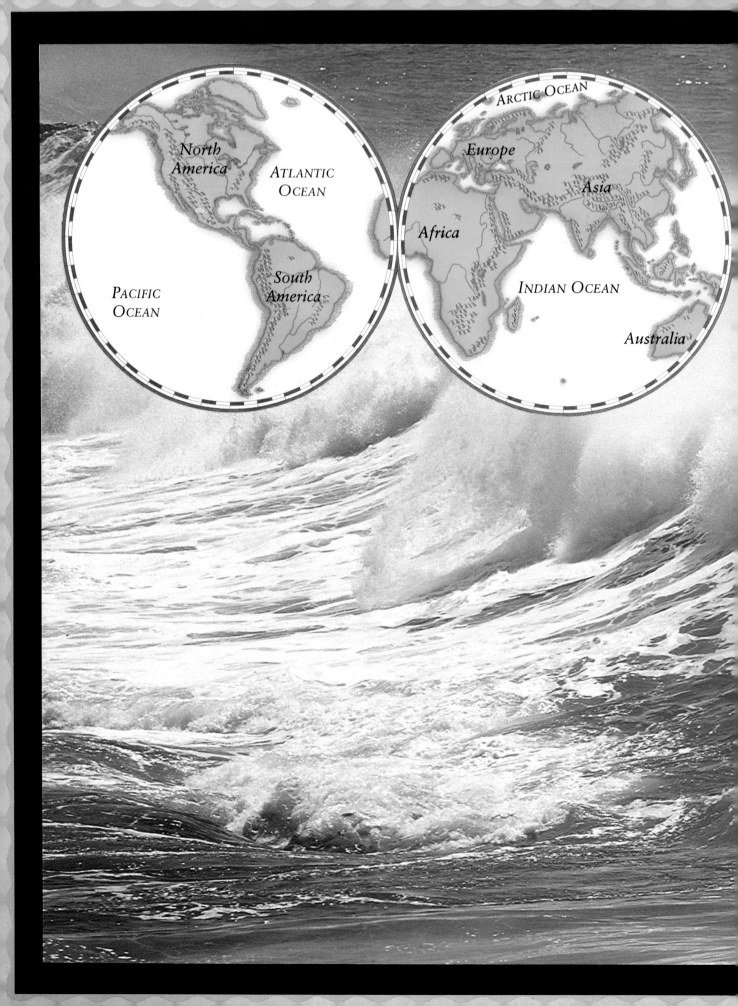

Chapter Three
THE OCEAN DEEP

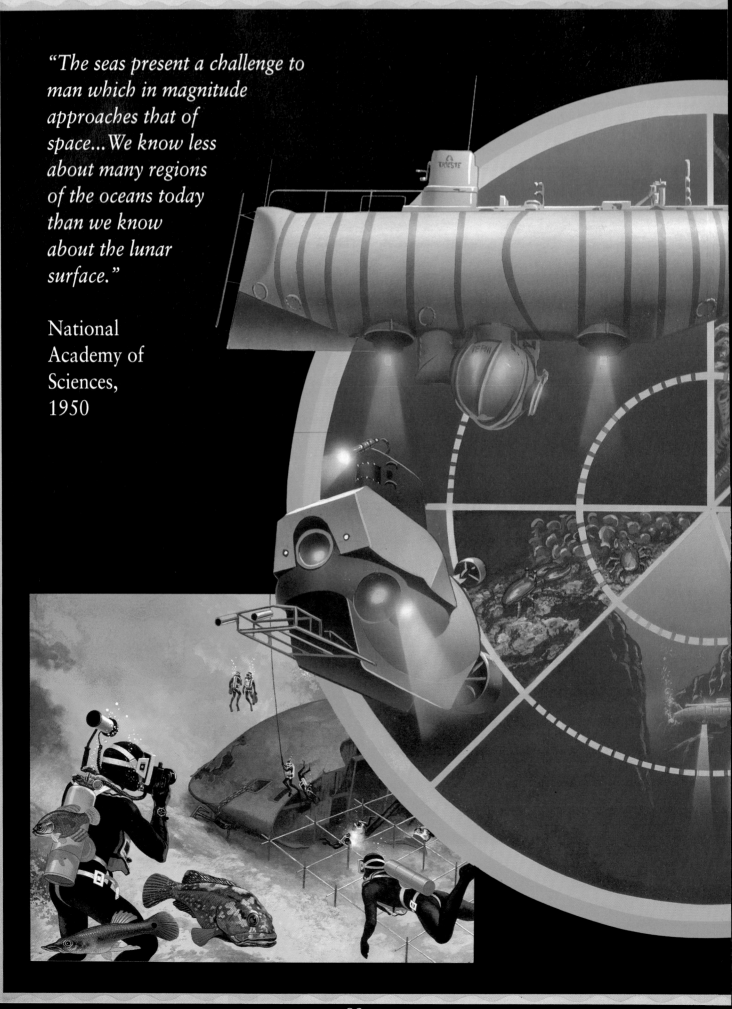

"The seas present a challenge to man which in magnitude approaches that of space... We know less about many regions of the oceans today than we know about the lunar surface."

National
Academy of
Sciences,
1950

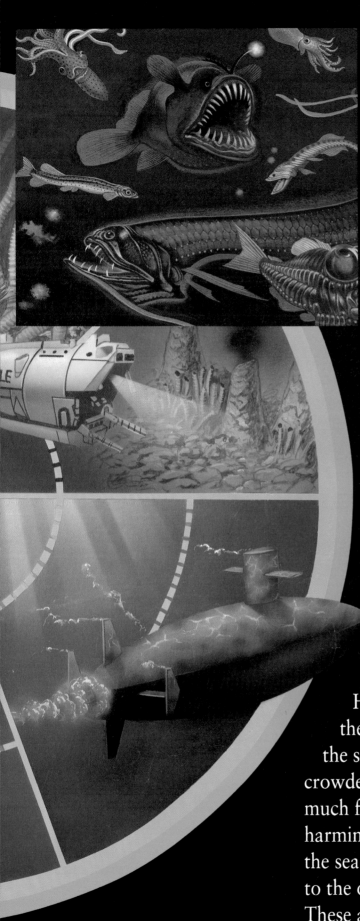

Introduction to
THE OCEAN DEEP

Perhaps our world should have been called "Planet Ocean" and not "Planet Earth." After all, more than two-thirds of its surface is covered by water. Scientists have worked out that the oceans contain about 529 million cubic miles of water! That's a lot of ocean to explore.

When Neil Armstrong stood on the Moon in 1969, only one successful mission had ever been made to the deepest part of the oceans. No one has returned there since. The secrets of the ocean depths are not easy to solve, but many people have been willing to try. In the 20th century, huge advances have been made in the development of exploration methods, but many questions remain. How did the oceans form and why are they so salty? Will people ever live under the sea? As our world becomes more crowded, we must understand our oceans. How much food can we take from the sea without harming it? How can we use our wastes to feed the sea rather than pollute it? What will happen to the oceans if "global warming" continues? These are just some of the many questions and mysteries facing today's marine scientists.

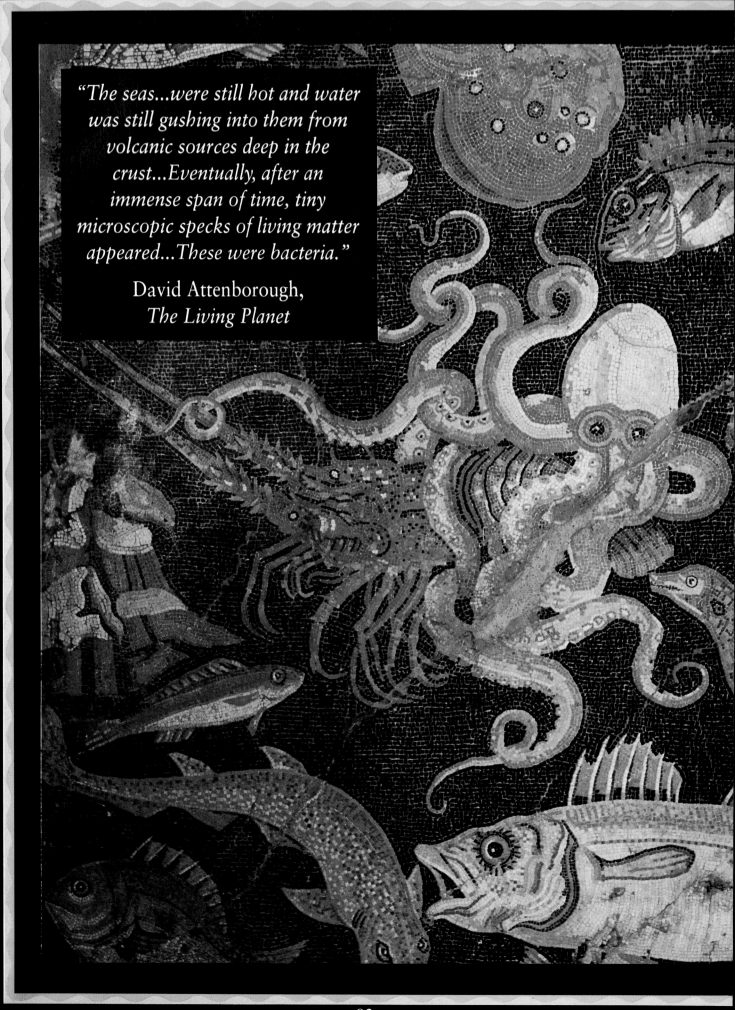

"*The seas...were still hot and water was still gushing into them from volcanic sources deep in the crust...Eventually, after an immense span of time, tiny microscopic specks of living matter appeared...These were bacteria.*"

David Attenborough,
The Living Planet

The Mysterious
W A T E R S

Today, thanks to underwater video cameras, people can travel the oceans without even getting wet. Modern ships, submarines, diving equipment, and satellite technology allow us to see into and explore the ocean's depths.

Early explorers braved the oceans with no real maps or communications systems. The Romans were accurate observers, as we know from their mosaics of Mediterranean fish and other sea creatures.

Until about 150 years ago, scientists believed that nothing could live in the deepest depths of the oceans, and that the deep seabed was covered in ice. But in 1860, a communications cable that ran under the Mediterranean Sea, at a depth of 1.3 miles (2 km), was brought to the surface for repairs. Growing on it were beautiful deep-sea corals. In modern times, deep-sea dredges have brought up a variety of ocean creatures from as far below the surface as 3.8 miles (6 km).

The First MYSTERIES

FIRST PAST THE POST
In 1773, Constantine John Phipps used a weighted line to measure a depth of over 0.6 miles (1 km) in the waters between Iceland and Norway, from his ship, H.M.S Racehorse.

Until two centuries ago, people believed that the oceans were bottomless and full of huge, hideous monsters. In the 18th century, however, scientists and explorers began to carry out experiments which helped them to find the bottom of the ocean.

Since 1920, scientists have used echo sounders to measure depth anywhere in the ocean in a matter of seconds and to show them what the seabed looks like. Divers can even carry their own small, waterproof echo sounders to tell them how far above the seabed they are. Even so, many mysteries and myths remain.

How big are the oceans?
Seas and oceans cover about 140,000,000 sq miles (362,000,000 sq km) of our planet, with an average depth of 2.3 miles (3.7 km). The biggest ocean is the Pacific, which measures 64,000,000 sq miles (166,000,000 sq km); the smallest is the Arctic Ocean, at 4,600,000 sq miles (12,000,000 sq km).

MAGICAL MERMAIDS
No one knows how the legends of mermaids began, but they have been told for centuries. The Spanish explorer Christopher Columbus (1451–1506) thought dugongs or sea cows (right) may have inspired the myth.

LIFE IN THE DEPTHS?
Scientists now know that life can exist on the seabed even in the deepest part of the ocean, the Mariana Trench. This was examined in 1995 by Kaiko (left), a Japanese crewless submarine. It is operated by cables from the surface and has brought back samples and pictures.

THE CHALLENGE OF THE OCEANS

In 1872, H.M.S. Challenger set off on a worldwide voyage of scientific research. For over three years, the ship's scientists mapped the seabed by taking depth soundings using a line and a lead ball. They tested mud and water and found over 4,000 new species of animals and plants. Their work filled 50 books and solved many mysteries.

Gods of the sea
Seafaring peoples have worshiped sea gods and goddesses for thousands of years. Rituals and ceremonies to please such gods are still practiced in some cultures today. Each major civilization had sea gods, such as Poseidon in ancient Greece and the Roman god Neptune (right). The crests on waves were believed by the Romans to be the white horses that pulled Neptune's chariot (top).

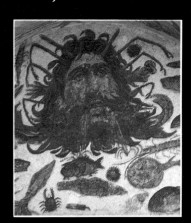

WHIRLING WATERS
Whirlpools form where strong tidal currents meet in narrow stretches of water, such as between Italy and Sicily in the Mediterranean Sea. Ancient Greek sailors called this whirlpool Charybdis and thought it was caused by a monster sucking in and spitting out the water.

THE LOST ISLAND
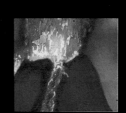
Even today no one knows if the continent of Atlantis ever existed. The ancient Greek writer Plato described a mythical island that was engulfed by waves. In about 1500 B.C., a volcanic eruption and earthquake on the island of Thira (now Santorini) had caused tidal waves and flooding. This event may have started the legend.

Changing VIEWS

The early explorers of the oceans must have been very brave. They had ships powered only by sails, and navigated using the stars and the Sun. They had no accurate maps and some believed that they might fall off the edge of the world. Explorers like Christopher Columbus, Ferdinand Magellan, and James Cook mapped out the ocean surfaces and the continents. Now scientists are starting to chart the world of mountains, trenches, and plains deep beneath the oceans. By drilling into the seabed, they are even able to work out how the oceans and continents were formed and where they will be in a million years!

Do the oceans stay the same size?
The size of our oceans is changing all the time, because of the constant, slow movements of the Earth's tectonic plates (see page 87) which pull the continents apart. For example, the Atlantic Ocean grows about 1.6 in (4 cm) wider every year. Other oceans and seas are widening very gradually, for the same reasons.

THE FLAT EARTH

For many centuries, people thought the Earth was flat and they could fall off the edge! In the 6th century B.C., the Greek mathematician Pythagoras (below) proved that the Earth was a sphere. Satellite pictures now allow us to look at our spherical world. But some people still insist that it is flat!

THE FIRST AROUND-THE-WORLD VOYAGE, 1522

FINDING A LINK
The Portuguese sailor Ferdinand Magellan crossed the Pacific Ocean in 1520. Before this, people had thought that India and America were joined by land. In 1522, one of his ships was the first to sail around the world, finally proving that the Earth was spherical.

MAPPING THE WORLD

Some ancient peoples had strange ideas about the Earth's shape! In about A.D. 50, Pomponius Mela from Rome drew a "wheel map" of a flat Earth surrounded by an ocean and divided by seas.

OCEAN SPINES

The Atlantic Ocean covers the Mid-Atlantic Ridge, a long chain of mountains up to 7.6 miles (4 km) high. It juts out in places to form islands like Iceland. There are ridges like this under all the oceans.

DRILLING DEEP

The Glomar Challenger *(left) has helped to solve the mystery of how the ocean floor was formed and how old it is. A drill digs into the seabed to collect samples of rock and silt. It can work in water up to 4.5 miles (7 km) deep.*

THE WHOLE PICTURE

The first world atlas, Theatrum Orbis Terrarum, *was published in 1570 by a Flemish map-maker, Abraham Ortelius. It contained maps which had been specially drawn for the book. It was very popular, but very inaccurate!*

The changing Earth

Scientists now believe that the oceans and continents sit on separate pieces, or tectonic plates (below), of the Earth's outer crust. About 250 million years ago, the continents were all joined together in a vast landmass known as *Pangaea*. Many plates have gradually pulled apart, moving the continents. They are still moving today. Some of the plates have collided, pushing up mountain ranges like the Himalayas.

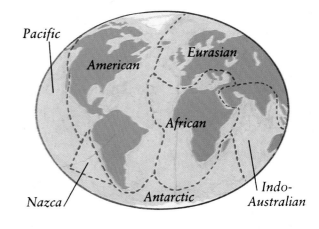

Pacific

American

Eurasian

African

Nazca

Antarctic

Indo-Australian

"*I experimented with all possible maneuvers of the Aqua-Lung: loops, somersaults and barrel rolls. I stood upside down on one finger and burst out laughing – a shrill, distorted laugh...Delivered from gravity and buoyancy, I flew around in space...*"

Jacques Cousteau, underwater explorer

The Lure of the
OCEANS

Most of us are fascinated by the ocean. For thousands of years, fishermen, coastal peoples, and seafarers have made their living from it and have had ways of life that revolve around it. Many people visit it on vacation for a few weeks each year. Others venture into it in search of pearls and other natural treasures.

By the 19th century, natural history had become popular. Early naturalists began to explore the mysterious animals and plants of the seashore. Some even ventured a short way underwater with buckets over their heads! Marine laboratories were built next to the sea in places like Naples in Italy and Plymouth in England. After World War II (1939–1945), underwater explorers, like Hans and Lottie Hass from Austria and Jacques Cousteau from France, began to take pictures of the strange worlds found beyond the seashore. Today, there are many underwater expeditions, which find more and more mysterious creatures every year.

The First DIVERS

People have been diving in the sea for thousands of years, to search for valuable sponges and pearls or fish and other food. The earliest divers had no equipment, but with practice could dive to 60–100 feet (20–30 m) while holding their breath. As the centuries passed, curiosity and the hope of finding treasure or defeating enemies led to the development of all kinds of diving aids. Even the Italian artist and inventor Leonardo da Vinci (1452–1519) designed a device for breathing underwater, although he never tried it. Today, thousands of people enjoy diving as a sport.

Where do pearls come from?
A pearl is formed when an irritating particle of sand gets into a shell. It is covered in smooth *nacre* (mother-of-pearl) to stop the itch. Many shellfish can form pearls, but valuable pearls come only from tropical seas. The biggest pearl ever found weighs over 13 lb (6 kg) and came from a giant clam.

NATURE'S DIVERS
Human efforts to explore the oceans must seem puny to the great sperm whales. They can hold their breath for at least an hour and dive down to over 0.6 miles (1 km) to hunt giant squid.

JEWELS OF THE SEA
Some of the first human divers were pearl and sponge collectors. Pearls have been gathered in the Arabian Gulf since at least 3000 B.C. Early divers wore tortoise-shell nose clips to keep water out of their nostrils.

UNDER THE SEAS

The astronomer Edmund Halley invented the first diving bell in 1690. Divers sat in a wooden cask with an open bottom. As the cask was lowered, the air inside was squashed by the rising water, so extra air was pumped in from wooden barrels. Divers could walk outside the bell with small casks over their heads.

THE HELMET SUIT

The first diving suit was developed in 1837 by Augustus Siebe from Germany. The watertight rubber suit had a heavy copper helmet which kept the diver on the seabed. Air was pumped down from the surface. This allowed divers to work at over 300 feet (90 m) deep. A very similar but lighter suit is now used by commercial divers.

Getting the bends

Early divers suffered from a strange, often fatal disease – decompression sickness, or the bends. If divers surface too fast, the decrease in pressure makes the nitrogen gas in their blood form bubbles, which block the blood's flow. Dive computers can work out the safest ascent speed. Divers with the bends go into decompression chambers (right), with high air pressure to make the gas dissolve.

DIVING ALONE

In 1865, Benoît Rouquayrol and Auguste Denayrouze invented a diving set that did not need an air hose from the surface. Air was carried in a canister and fed through a valve in the helmet. But the set could be used only in shallow water at low pressure.

DIVING TODAY

Modern SCUBA (Self-Contained Underwater Breathing Apparatus) gives divers great freedom. The Aqua-Lung, the first breathing device to let people dive independently, was invented in the 1940s. The explorers Jacques Cousteau and Frédéric Dumas developed the demand valve, which gives air to divers when they breathe in (rather than all the time, which wastes air).

Mysterious CREATURES

The number of sea creatures roaming the seas is truly amazing. Among the most spectacular ocean dwellers are the great whales, sharks, and manta rays. In the past, they were seen only as a source of food and money and many were hunted and killed. Now scientists are trying to unravel the mysterious lives of these enormous creatures, in the hope of saving them from extinction.

Today, it is possible for everyone to see some of these amazing animals in the wild. Many travel agencies now offer whale and dolphin watching trips, coral-reef safaris, and trips in glass-bottomed boats, while more and more people are learning to scuba dive.

MONSTERS OF THE DEEP
Early seafarers lived in constant fear of the hideous monsters that were believed to lurk in the ocean. Sixteenth-century books and maps show fish and reptiles with huge heads and fangs and long, writhing serpents. Such beliefs persisted well into the 19th century.

Ruler of the seas
The blue whale is the largest animal on Earth. It can grow up to 100 feet (30 m) long – bigger than most of the dinosaurs. Yet this giant mammal eats shrimps called *krill* that are just 2 in (5 cm) long. Each whale swallows about 4 million krill every day!

SHARK ATTACK!

Films like Jaws *have given the great white shark a reputation as a terrifying killer. With its huge jaws and sharp teeth, it can tear a person apart. Little is known about the life of this monster and scientists are trying to find out more. But people have killed more sharks than sharks have killed people – and this huge predator is now an endangered species.*

How great is the great white shark? Most great white sharks can grow to more than 20 feet (6 m) long. In 1959, Alfred Dean caught the largest fish ever taken with a rod, off the coast of Australia. It was a great white weighing 664 lb (1,209.5 kg). The biggest great white ever caught was also caught off the Australian coast, in 1976, by Clive Green. It weighed 3,338 lb (1,537 kg). Australian Rodney Fox survived a great white shark attack in 1963. He had hundreds of stitches and still has scars from his waist to his neck.

LARVAE ALERT

In 1763, leaf-shaped fish were found in the Sargasso Sea and named Leptocephalus. A century later, it was proved that they were young freshwater eels. The eels lay their eggs in the sea, and the larvae travel to North America and Europe, where they swim into rivers.

MEGALODON

DEADLY GIANTS

Early Mediterranean peoples believed that fossilized sharks' teeth were snakes' tongues, turned to stone when St. Paul visited Malta in

GREAT WHITE

A.D. 60. *Some teeth are 5 in (12 cm) long and suggest a huge, extinct shark, Megalodon, which could have been 100 feet (30 m) long!*

THE DEVIL'S CREATURES

The strange "horns" on the manta ray's head have earned it the name of "devil-fish." Until the 1920s, it was thought to be a dangerous predator. Divers now swim happily with

these giants. Despite its huge size, the manta feeds only on floating plankton (tiny organisms). The "horns" help to direct plankton-rich water into its mouth.

"Now and then I felt a slight vibration and an apparent slackening off of the cable. Word came that a cross-swell had arisen...We were swinging at 3,028 feet, and, would we come up?"

William Beebe, on his record bathysphere descent in 1934.

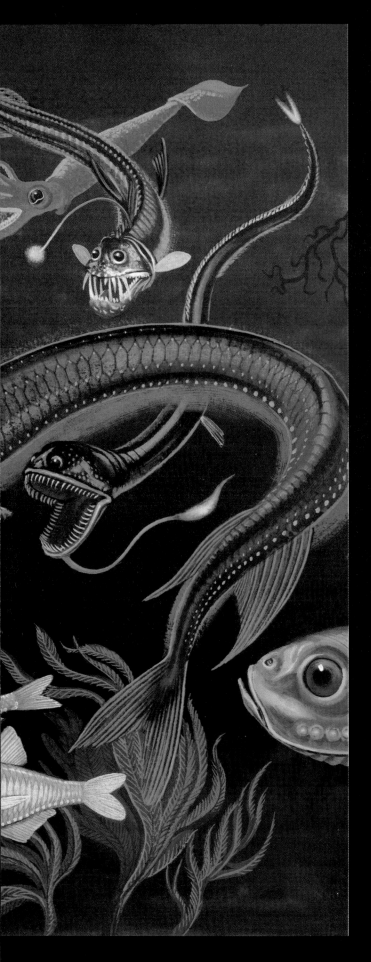

The Deepest DEPTHS

A thousand yards down in the ocean depths, the sea is icy cold. It is pitch black and the water pressure is strong enough to crush a person like an eggshell. These are the problems faced both by underwater explorers and by the animals that live here.

The animals solve such problems in ingenious ways. Most deep-sea fish have luminous body parts with which to hunt and find mates. Some squid even squirt luminous "ink" (fluid) to confuse predators. Food is scarce in the depths; most fish have huge jaws and expandable stomachs and can eat prey which is at least as big as they are. The males of some species are attached to the females, to make sure the females have mates.

The explorers are protected by submersibles (submarines) made from strong materials. They carry food and water and are well heated. They also have powerful lights so that the crew can see the water around them.

Ocean Trenches & VENTS

HITTING THE BOTTOM
On January 23, 1960,
Navy Lt. Donald
Walsh and Jacques
Piccard dived into the ocean's
deepest trench, the Mariana, in the
bathyscaph Trieste. They reached
the bottom over 4 hours later,
after traveling nearly
7 miles (11 km).

Like the urge to climb the highest mountains on Earth, people have always wanted to dive deeper and explore the "inner space" of the oceans. In the last thirty years, deep-sea research submarines have made this possible. Most of these can operate down to less than one mile deep, but much of the ocean floor lies below this. The *Trieste* voyage in 1960 is the only time people have ever descended to the deepest part of the ocean. With such submersibles, scientists have discovered underwater volcanoes, hot-water vents, and many previously unimagined animals.

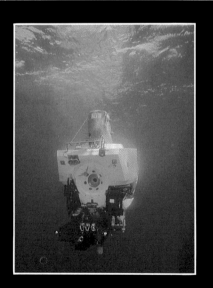

Exploring the seabed

Today, scientists can explore the deep seabed in small submersibles like the *Alvin*, built in 1964. They use instruments that measure, film, and collect the water and animals around the craft. It moves freely, but it cannot go much deeper than 2.4 miles (4 km). The *Alvin* discovered marine life around deep-sea vents (see page 97).

OASES OF LIFE

In the deep ocean, the water is icy cold. But hot springs may escape from volcanic cracks, or vents, in the seabed. In 1977, scientists explored a vent 1.3 miles (2 km) down, near the Galapagos Islands.

It was teeming with tube worms, mussels, crabs, and fish, feeding on bacteria and each other. The bacteria get their energy from the sulfurous gases and minerals that come out of the vents. So the whole food web depends on chemical energy rather than sunlight.

BLACK SMOKERS

The *Nautile* has found deep-sea vents near Mexico, in which tall chimneys of hardened minerals have built up. Hot water gushes out at temperatures of up to 730 °F. As it rises from the surrounding rock, the water reacts with the minerals and turns black, pouring out of the chimney like smoke.

MODERN SUBMERSIBLES

The giants of the submarine world are the nuclear craft. Small research submersibles can stay submerged for only a few days, but nuclear submarines remain underwater for up to 2 years. They are bigger than most passenger ships and carry large crews.

DEEP DOWN

The deepest spot on Earth is the 7-mile Challenger Deep in the Pacific Ocean's Mariana Trench (see page 96). The water pressure at the bottom is an astounding 1.25 tons per square yard.

Which is the highest underwater mountain? The biggest known mountain under the surface of the sea is Mount Kea, underneath the Pacific Ocean. It climbs to a massive 6 miles (10 km) above the sea floor. It is therefore almost 1.2 miles (2 km) higher than Mount Everest, the tallest mountain on land – yet it is still invisible from the surface of the ocean!

The Living
DEPTHS

GIANT JAWS

"Megamouth," the most mysterious of all sharks, was first hauled up from deep water in 1976. It can be 15 feet (4.5 m) long and weighs at least 1,650 lb (750 kg). With its huge mouth and tiny teeth, it eats only small creatures. What a relief!

One of the greatest challenges to scientists is finding out what mysterious creatures live in the depths of the oceans. Delicate animals like jellyfish simply break apart as they are hauled to the surface, because the temperature and pressure changes on the way up are too great for their fragile bodies.

In recent years, many new species have been collected using sensitive robotic arms on submersibles. With these machines, the scientists can gently place the animals in special protective containers before taking them out of the water. Finding an animal that no one has ever seen before is very exciting!

How deep can fish swim?
The deepest that a fish has been caught is at 5 miles (8 km) beneath the surface of the Atlantic Ocean. The fish was a type of eel and was caught by Dr. Gilbert L. Voss in 1970. A living creature has been seen even further down, at 7 miles (11 km) under the Pacific Ocean. It was probably a flat sea cucumber.

CLEAN UP!
Over 0.6 miles (1 km) down in all the major oceans, there are great "deserts" of soft mud, kept clean by deep-sea vacuum cleaners! These sea cucumbers feed by sucking up mud, full of the dead remains of creatures from above.

DEEP-SEA DWELLERS
*Dive deeper than
about 2,000 feet (600 m) in the sea
and you will find yourself in a world of
darkness, broken by strange flashes of light.*

*Deep-sea fish carry luminous lamps
on their bodies to help them hunt
and catch prey. Fish of the same
species can recognize each other from
their particular light patterns.*

A living fossil?

The coelacanth looks more like a reptile than a fish. Before 1938, only fossilized coelacanths more than 70 million years old had been found. In that year, a live specimen was caught and taken to a museum in South Africa. Sadly, this "living fossil" may soon become extinct. Only a few hundred remain, living at depths of 495–990 feet (150–300 m) near the Comoro Islands between Madagascar and Mozambique.

MYSTERIOUS HUES
*Sunlight consists of rainbow
colors. In water, each color
only travels to a certain
depth. Red stops first, so red animals look
almost black in the depths. Many deep-sea
creatures, like prawns (above) and sea
spiders (below), are red, for camouflage in
their dark world.*

JELLYFISH
*Many kinds of
jellyfish and similar
animals live in the
ocean depths. Some are
large, like the lion's mane
jellyfish which grows to 6.6 feet
(2 m) across its bell (body).
Others are tiny. Many glow
with bright colors as they
move, and stun other
creatures with stinging
tentacles like those of the
compass jellyfish (left).*

"Then, directly in front of us, there it was: an endless slab of rusted steel rising out of the bottom – the massive hull of the Titanic! I felt like a space voyager peering at an alien city wall on some empty planet."

Robert Ballard, marine scientist

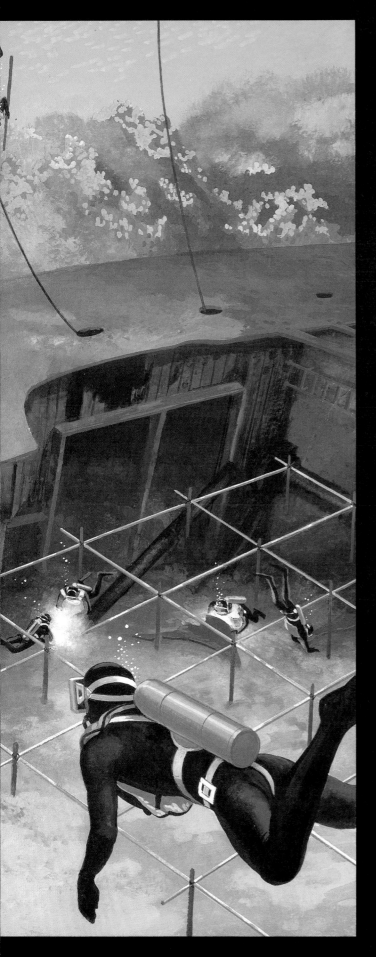

Treasures of
THE DEEP

Over the centuries there have been many shipwrecks, and much treasure has been lost in the ocean depths. Today, with the help of technology, some of these valuables are coming to the surface again. Robot submersibles with video cameras can be sent to find treasure and to help scientists work out ways of recovering it.

Amateur divers enjoy exploring wrecks and many have helped to uncover archaeological "treasures." The famous wreck of the *Mary Rose* was recovered almost entirely by volunteers. In 1995, divers finished excavating a 3,313-year-old Bronze Age wreck in the Mediterranean Sea. Such "time capsules" have taught us a lot about our past. Wrecks can survive in the sea for thousands of years because they are preserved by mud or sand. This also makes them difficult to find! Archaeologists must dig away the sediment carefully, just as they do on land.

Underwater
H U N T S

Many people dream of finding sunken treasure...but few have succeeded. Time, money, and equipment are needed to do so. However, finding treasure has been made much easier with modern technology. Once treasure is found, it is possible to go back to an exact spot in the sea using a Global Positioning System. This takes readings from satellites in space and is accurate to within a few yards.

Not all treasure is made of gold – 24,000 valuable plates were raised from a wreck called the *Diana* in 1994. The ship sank near Singapore in 1817 in only 106 feet (32 m) of water, but was quickly buried in sand.

RAISING THE PAST
The flagship of King Henry VIII of England, the Mary Rose, *was raised from the English seabed in 1982. It sank in 1545, and has told historians a lot about life in Tudor times. It was pulled up by the* Tor Mog, *the biggest lifting barge in existence.*

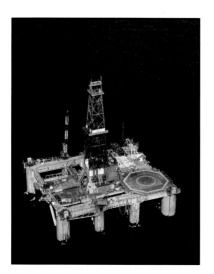

Liquid riches
Oil is known as the sea's "black gold." Countries like Saudi Arabia and Brunei have become rich by collecting oil from beneath their seas. Most oil rigs can work only in less than 660 feet (200 m) of water. Now special drilling ships are finding oil in much deeper places. Computers keep the ship in the right spot while it drills through the seabed.

SEARCHING FOR WRECKS

Many wrecks are found by sonar equipment (left). Waves of sound are sent to the seabed. When they bounce back, the pattern they make shows up lumps and bumps.

What is the oldest shipwreck?
The oldest known wreck dates from the 14th century B.C., and still lies off the coast of Turkey.
Do the oceans contain any other natural treasures?
Sea water contains tiny amounts of gold, but not enough to be extracted (unfortunately!). Other valuable elements, such as magnesium and bromine, can be taken from the water.

A TERRIBLE DISASTER

In 1912, the biggest ocean liner ever, the Titanic, collided with an iceberg. Over 1,500 people died as the ship sank to the seabed, 2.4 miles (4 km) below. It was found in 1985 (below), using hi-tech equipment. Submersibles have since taken scientists to see the sad remains.

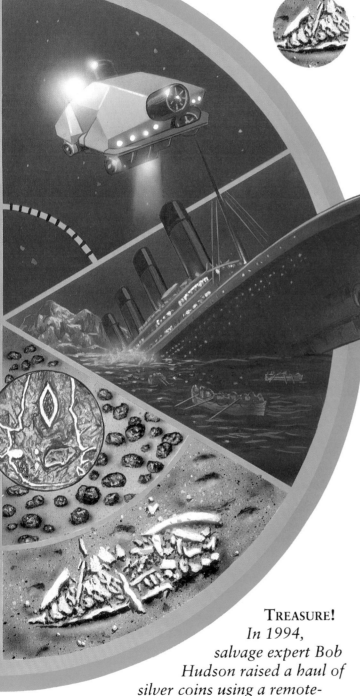

TREASURE!

In 1994, salvage expert Bob Hudson raised a haul of silver coins using a remote-controlled grab. They came from the John Barry, a ship sunk by a torpedo in the Arabian Sea in 1944. Other recent finds have included gold bars and valuable pottery.

NATURE'S GIFTS

Manganese nodules are found on the seabed below about 2.5 miles (4 km). They contain valuable metals such as copper and nickel and take millions of years to form. Specialized mining systems are being developed to collect them.

Exploring the DEPTHS

The early films of Hans and Lottie Hass and Jacques Cousteau allowed many people to explore the wonders of the underwater world on their own TV sets. Now, with modern diving suits and camera equipment, ordinary people can plunge into the oceans and examine their watery secrets for themselves. Louis Boutan, the inventor of the first underwater camera, would have been amazed to see the disposable waterproof cameras now for sale. Some resorts now offer submarine trips rather than boat tours. Soon you may be able to buy a submersible of your own!

PRESSURE SUITS
Wearing some diving suits feels like wearing a submarine! The Wasp and Jim (left) are popular designs, in which a diver can reach 1,650 feet (500 m) with enough air for three days. However, the suits are expensive and clumsy to use.

Do submarines ever get lost?
On September 1, 1973, a small submersible, the *Pisces III*, was rescued from 1,580 feet (480 m) below sea level. Two men had been trapped inside for three days, after losing control of the craft and straying out of radio contact with their surface ship. It took two crewed submersibles and a robot vehicle to find and recover the submarine.

OCEAN FLYERS
Deep Flight One *(above) is a new craft that "flies" underwater. It is very strong, but weighs only as much as a large car. Deep Flight Two may soon take people down to the depths more easily than the clumsy Trieste.*

FISHING THE DEEP

Scientists can catch animals from the deep-sea floor by using special underwater sleds with nets. The sled is towed by a ship over the muddy seabed, on the end of a cable up to 9 miles (15 km) long. It can carry instruments to examine the water, and video or still cameras.

SNAPPING THE OCEANS

Scientists have started dropping their cameras into the sea! The Bathysnap *(left)* is a special camera that sinks to the seabed and takes pictures of the mysterious animals that live deep down. When the film is finished, the camera is automatically released from the heavy weights which hold it and floats to the surface.

Say "Cheese!"

Louis Boutan took the first underwater photograph in 1893 *(left)*, but his camera was heavy and clumsy. Today's cameras are small and light and have brought many of the ocean's mysteries to life. Special lamps emphasize colors and scenery. Remote-controlled still and video cameras can explore the seabed, sending back images to scientists on research ships. These pictures can be transmitted live to laboratories and museums worldwide.

YELLOW SUBMARINE

The British scientist Robert Leeds has recently designed a small "yellow submarine" *(right)*, shaped like a flying saucer, for commercial use.

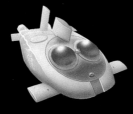

It will be tested in 1996 and, if it is declared safe, you may soon be able to hire one and go fish-watching down to a depth of 165 feet (50 m).

"It is true that we are destroying an extraordinary world we scarcely know, almost without thinking. Yet there are many ways to stop this happening...we cannot put off action until tomorrow."

Greenpeace

The Future of the OCEANS

Our oceans will face all sorts of problems in the future. When the *Exxon Valdez* tanker was wrecked in the Arctic Ocean in 1989, it lost 35,000 tons of oil. Thousands of birds, otters, fish, and shore animals were killed. Every year, 20 billion tons of environmentally damaging substances are dumped into the ocean, while many sea birds, dolphins, and turtles are trapped in nets meant to catch squid, and die. Fish are being taken from the sea faster than they can replace themselves.

However, if we are able to solve these problems, the oceans hold an exciting future for us. Astronauts have lived for up to a year in space. Soon we should be able to do the same in the sea. So far, aquanauts have only lived underwater for a few weeks, but who knows – one day we might build and inhabit underwater cities. Our future may depend upon our oceans. We must look after them.

Inhabiting the OCEANS

People have always dreamed of living underwater. Many fantastic stories have been written about "human fish" and underwater cities. The first steps have been taken toward making this dream come true. Scientists have developed a membrane that keeps water out but allows oxygen to pass in. It has been tried successfully on rabbits. Could it one day allow humans to breathe freely underwater? Divers are already able to live for some time in "underwater homes," or saturation habitats. These are small and cramped but, one day, larger underwater homes may be created, in which people can live and work for many months or even several years.

BREATHING UNDER THE SEA
In the 1960s, scientist Waldemar Ayres used a special membrane to take oxygen from sea water through artificial "gills." He breathed underwater for over an hour. No one has yet used his system for diving.

WATERY HOUSES
The first "underwater home" for divers was the Conshelf I, *invented by Jacques Cousteau. In 1962, two divers spent a week in it at a depth of 33 feet (10 m). Sealab (right) and Tektite are habitats in which people have lived for up to 30 days at depths of nearly 660 feet (200 m).*

AN ICY ENVIRONMENT
Even the cold waters of the Arctic and Antarctic are being explored by diving scientists. They have discovered giant sea spiders, anemones, and fish with antifreeze in their blood.

FARMING THE OCEANS

Many countries have sea farms where fish, shrimps, shellfish, (right), and seaweeds are cultivated for food. At present, these are mostly established in shallow water where they can be looked after easily. One day, it may be possible to farm deep-sea fish with diver-farmers living in underwater farmhouses.

How long can people hold their breath underwater?
Most people can hold their breath for about 30 seconds. In December 1994, Francesco "Pipin" Ferreras became the world breath-holding champion when he dived to 420 feet (127 m). He held his breath for 2 minutes, 26 seconds. **WARNING: THIS IS A VERY DANGEROUS THING TO DO AND SHOULD NOT BE TRIED.**

TAKING THE PLUNGE

Scuba gear means that almost anyone can learn to dive and explore the deep. But compressed air, used by most divers, is unsafe below about 165 feet (50 m).

Special mixtures of the gases nitrogen or helium and oxygen allow trained divers (left) to reach 330 feet (100 m). Below that, divers use a diving bell as a base, to work down to about 1,320 feet (400 m).

Cities of the future

Many books and films have explored the possibilities of humans living underwater in specially designed towns and cities. Already, a few travel agencies are experimenting with submerged hotels (right) from which guests can watch fish, snorkel, and scuba dive. But as the Earth's population increases, will underwater buildings have more serious uses? Will human colonies be able to live in the depths of the oceans?

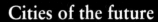

The Unsolved
MYSTERIES

Despite modern ships and scientific equipment, many ocean mysteries remain to be solved. Some, like eel migrations, have been partly explained by observations over many years. Many ancient legends of sea serpents were probably inspired by sightings of rare creatures like the oarfish. Tales of battles between giant sea serpents and whales may be true, because sperm whales eat giant squid. But not all the stories can be explained. Who knows what other creatures may still lurk in the dark depths of the ocean?

A TANGLE OF TENTACLES
When a giant octopus (below) spreads out its arms, you can fit two large cars between them. These huge creatures can be 11.5 feet (3.5 m) long. They are intelligent and shy and are rarely seen; no one knows just how big they can get.

Bermuda

Florida

Bahamas

ATLANTIC OCEAN

Cuba

Puerto Rico

WANDERING GIANTS
Every April, huge whale sharks appear off the Australian Barrier Reef. Basking sharks (left) leave the coasts of Europe in the winter, but no one knows where they go. The travels of these giants are being investigated using radio tags linked to satellites.

Are octopuses dangerous?
Some kinds are. The pretty blue-ringed octopus, found in Australia, is small – only 5–6 in (10–15 cm) – but its bite can kill a person in just a few minutes.

Octopuses have three hearts, but this does not make them particularly strong. They get tired very quickly and will give up a fight if it is too difficult.

MYSTERIOUS MIGRATIONS

Many marine animals make long migrations, but it is still a mystery how they find their way. People used to believe that the long hairs from a horse's tail turned into young eels

when they dropped into a river. The eels are now known to migrate to rivers for thousands of miles, from the Sargasso Sea (see page 93). How do they find their way? This is still a puzzling secret.

The fearsome Kraken

For centuries, people have told stories of the Kraken – a huge, octopus-like animal which can pull down a ship. These tales are probably based on giant squid, which can be 50 feet (15 m) long. Their tentacles may have been mistaken for sea serpents.

SNAKES ALIVE!

The strange oarfish grows to a staggering 25 feet (7 m) long and lives in deep water. With its bright red fins and "mane," it could be mistaken for a sea serpent.

But some sightings remain unexplained. In 1817, a huge "sea serpent" was seen in Massachusetts by many people over several weeks...but its identity is still a mystery.

THE DEADLY TRIANGLE

Over 70 ships and 20 planes are said to have vanished in the Bermuda Triangle in the Atlantic Ocean. Future searches may find these wrecks and explain their disappearance.

BLOBS ON THE BEACH

In the last century, huge, 5–10-ton "blobs" of dead sea creatures have been washed up worldwide. Could they be parts of unknown giant beasts?

The power of the ocean

As science and technology develop, scientists are able to unravel more and more of the secrets of our oceans. Yet humans still have a long way to go if we are to fully understand this mysterious, dark world ruled by giant monsters and amazing creatures – a world in which we will always be strangers.

6th century B.C. Pythagoras
proves Earth is round
c. 5000 B.C. Legends of fish-tailed
goddesses appear
c. 3000 B.C. First records of pearl diving
Ancient Egyptians invent sails
c. 1500 B.C. Volcanic eruption on Santorini
c. 750 B.C. Homer describes Charybdis
c. A.D. 50 Mela draws "wheel map" of Earth
c. 1300 Tortoise-shell goggles used
1520 Magellan discovers Pacific Ocean
1522 Magellan's ship sails around world
1570 Ortelius publishes Theatrum Orbis
Terrarum, the first world atlas
1690 Halley invents diving bell
1715 Early diving suit invented
1763 "Leptocephalus" found in Sargasso
Sea and thought to be strange fish
1773 Phipps takes depth sounding
1807 Steamboat invented
1837 Siebe invents helmet diving suit
1860 Life found on Mediterranean cable
1865 Rouquayrol and Denayrouze invent
independent diving set
1872 H.M.S. Challenger departs on voyage
1893 Boutan takes undersea photograph
1912 Titanic sinks
1915 Pangaea theory proposed
1920 Echo sounders first used
1930 Barton and Beebe's
bathysphere
dive

LINE

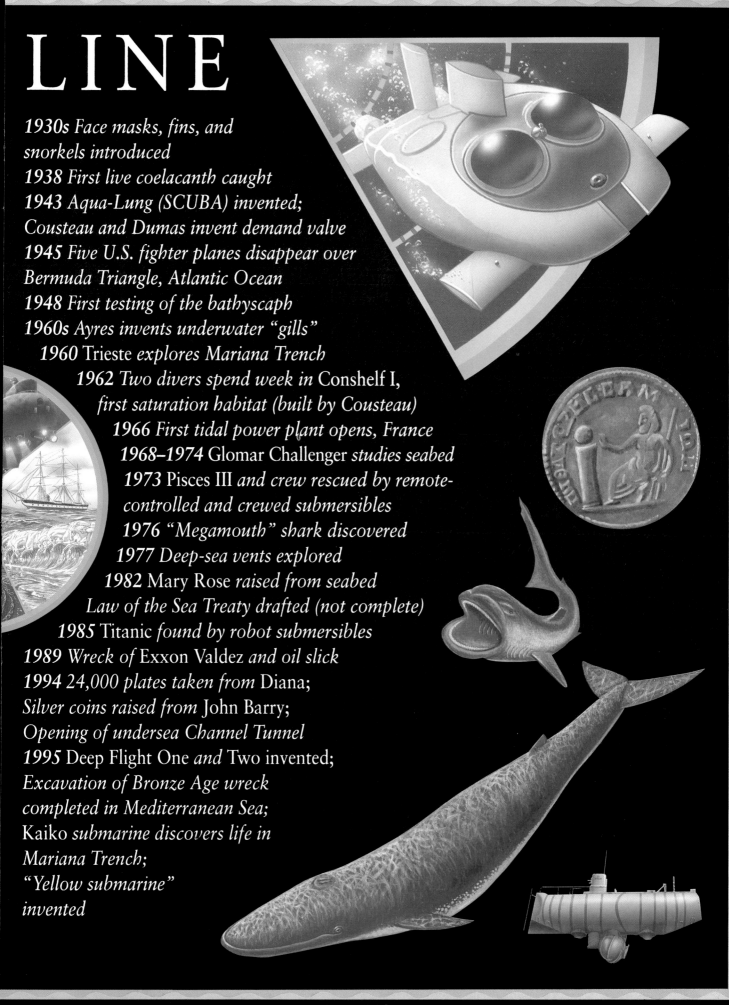

1930s *Face masks, fins, and snorkels introduced*

1938 *First live coelacanth caught*

1943 *Aqua-Lung (SCUBA) invented; Cousteau and Dumas invent demand valve*

1945 *Five U.S. fighter planes disappear over Bermuda Triangle, Atlantic Ocean*

1948 *First testing of the bathyscaph*

1960s *Ayres invents underwater "gills"*

1960 Trieste *explores Mariana Trench*

1962 *Two divers spend week in* Conshelf I, *first saturation habitat (built by Cousteau)*

1966 *First tidal power plant opens, France*

1968–1974 Glomar Challenger *studies seabed*

1973 Pisces III *and crew rescued by remote-controlled and crewed submersibles*

1976 *"Megamouth" shark discovered*

1977 *Deep-sea vents explored*

1982 Mary Rose *raised from seabed Law of the Sea Treaty drafted (not complete)*

1985 Titanic *found by robot submersibles*

1989 *Wreck of* Exxon Valdez *and oil slick*

1994 *24,000 plates taken from* Diana; *Silver coins raised from* John Barry; *Opening of undersea Channel Tunnel*

1995 *Deep Flight One and Two invented; Excavation of Bronze Age wreck completed in Mediterranean Sea;* Kaiko *submarine discovers life in Mariana Trench; "Yellow submarine" invented*

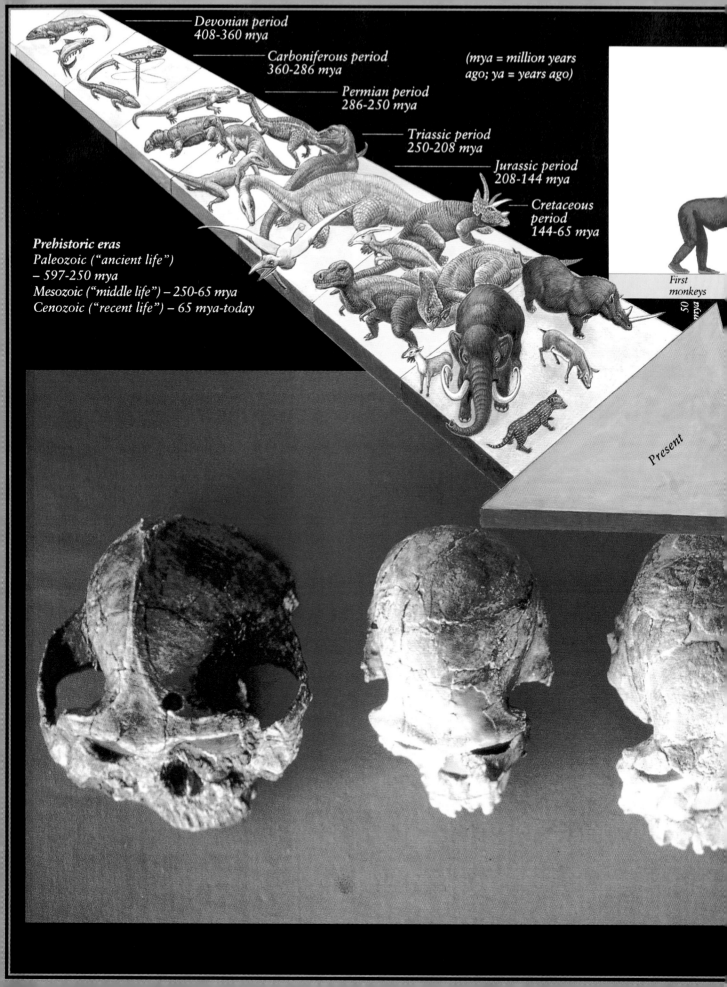

Devonian period
408-360 mya

Carboniferous period
360-286 mya

Permian period
286-250 mya

Triassic period
250-208 mya

Jurassic period
208-144 mya

Cretaceous
period
144-65 mya

*(mya = million years
ago; ya = years ago)*

Prehistoric eras
*Paleozoic ("ancient life")
– 597-250 mya
Mesozoic ("middle life") – 250-65 mya
Cenozoic ("recent life") – 65 mya-today*

First
monkeys

50
mya

Present

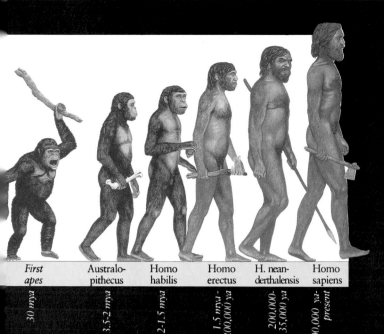

First apes — 30 mya

Australo-pithecus — 3.5-2 mya

Homo habilis — 2-1.5 mya

Homo erectus — 1.5 mya - 200,000 ya

H. nean-derthalensis — 200,000-35,000 ya

Homo sapiens — 200,000 ya - present

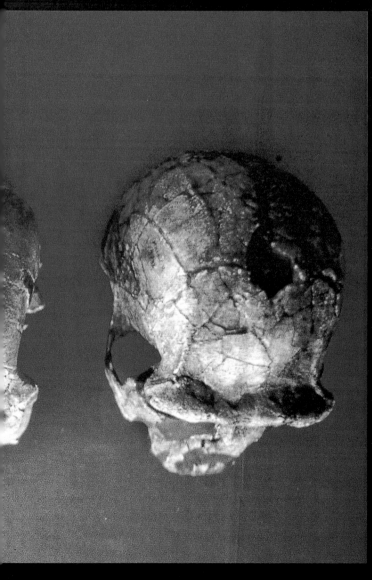

Chapter Four
PREHISTORIC LIFE

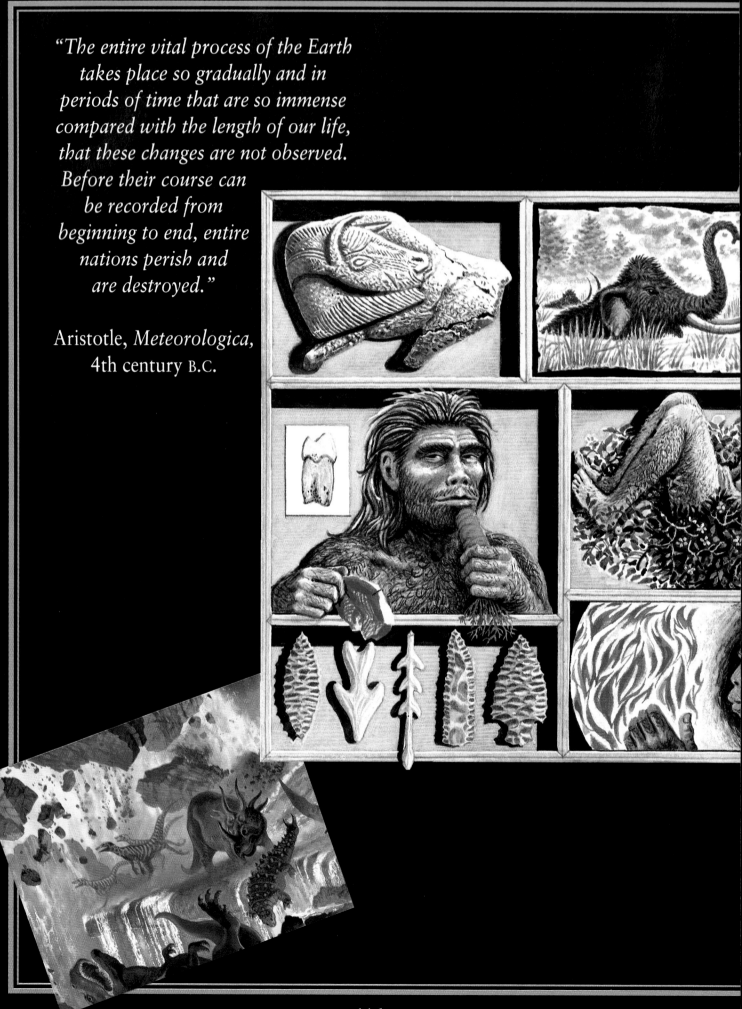

"The entire vital process of the Earth takes place so gradually and in periods of time that are so immense compared with the length of our life, that these changes are not observed. Before their course can be recorded from beginning to end, entire nations perish and are destroyed."

Aristotle, *Meteorologica*, 4th century B.C.

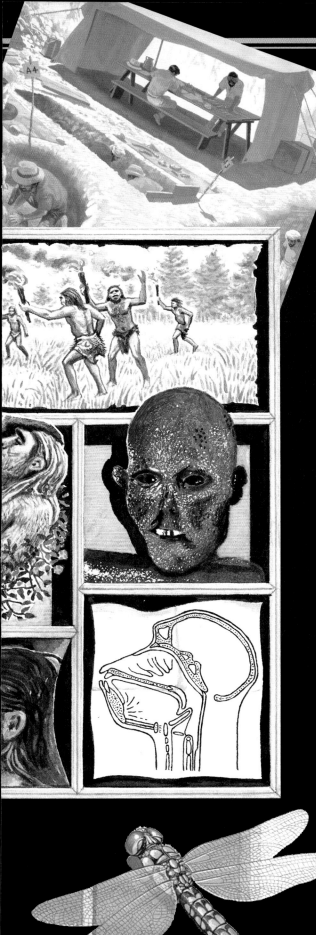

Introduction to PREHISTORIC LIFE

Humans have trodden the Earth for thousands of years, not knowing how old the planet is and how many past worlds lie beneath their feet. It was not until the 18th century that people realized that bones, shells, and coal found in rocks were the remains of prehistoric life – animals and plants that had lived before historical records started to be written.

Scientists then began a voyage of discovery, digging up dinosaurs, pterodactyls, mammoths, and even our ancestors. And the Earth still holds many surprises. Paleontologists (scientists who study prehistoric life) continue to find fossils that challenge their knowledge.

As information is gathered on extinct animals and plants, more branches are added to our map of the tree of life. But new discoveries also tell us how little we know. So far, we have found less than one percent of all the species that ever lived, and many puzzles remain unsolved. Why did the dinosaurs die out? How did life begin? Who were our ancestors? In deserts, under the seas, and sometimes even in our own backyards, scientists are exploring the past, solving old mysteries and finding many new ones.

"*You will observe by these remains The Creature had two sets of brains – One in his head (the usual place), the other in his spinal base.*"

B.L. Taylor, *Chicago Tribune,* on the discovery of *Stegasaurus,* 1912

What is a DINOSAUR?

Dinosaurs were an extraordinary group of animals that lived from 230 to 64 million years ago. They had upright limbs, stood erect, and swung their legs backward and forward, unlike reptiles or amphibians whose legs sprawl out to the side. There were some small dinosaurs, but most were large and some reached gigantic sizes, weighing 100 tons or more.

Dinosaurs were a diverse group of animals. Among the plant-eaters were nimble bipeds, armored ankylosaurs, and huge, plant-eating sauropods. These were hunted by meat-eating theropods, such as the dromaeosaurs and the fearsome *Tyrannosaurus*.

The dinosaur world was shared by many other groups. Ichthyosaurs and plesiosaurs – huge marine reptiles – dominated the seas, while winged pterosaurs flew through the skies. These and countless other animals and plants died out at the end of the Dinosaur Age, but some groups, such as birds and mammals, survived.

The First L I F E

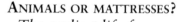

According to James Ussher in 1650, the Earth and its life were formed on October 22nd, 4004 B.C. We now know that the Earth is 4.5 billion years old and that life began over 3 billion years ago.

The first life was simple. More complex life-forms appeared 600 million years ago. The vertebrates began life in the seas as jawless fish. Plants invaded land first. Insects and amphibians followed, 400 million years ago. Reptiles evolved into dinosaurs and small, hairy creatures – the mammals.

PREHISTORIC PAPERWEIGHTS
Ammonites, often used as ornaments, are fossilized Mesozoic shelled squid.

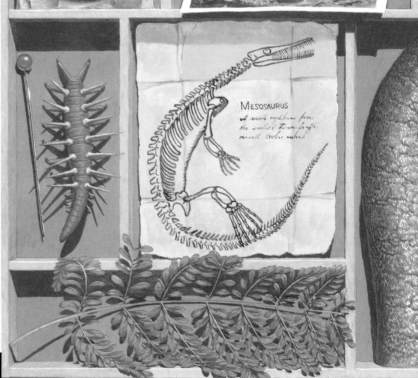

MESOSAURUS

THE GREENING OF THE EARTH
Plants were the very first organisms to colonize the land. Small, fernlike plants provided food and shelter for the earliest land animals, which included scorpions, spiders, insects, and even snails.

What is a vertebrate?
A vertebrate is any creature with a spinal column (backbone) and cranium (skull). The first vertebrates ashore were the amphibians, 400 million years ago. They used their fins as limbs and had eight toes (later reduced to 5). Creatures without a spinal column are known as invertebrates.

RAMPANT REPTILES
As they spread into many new habitats, the early land-living reptiles underwent a surge of development. Some, such as Mesosaurus (right), went back to the water; some adopted a hot-blooded lifestyle, evolved hair, and became mammals; others took to the air; one group became the ruling reptiles – the dinosaurs.

Jawless fish
The first vertebrates were small fish such as Astraspis (above). Instead of jaws, they had a simple mouth opening and sucked up their food, which consisted of waste matter such as dead creatures and plants from the ocean floor.

Birth and death of a species
The naturalist Charles Darwin (1809-1882) developed the theory of evolution. It states that species are constantly developing to cope with changes in food supply and climate; if not, they die out.

Triassic take-off
Reptiles invented flight more than 200 million years ago. Sharovipteryx (left) used a membranous wing, supported by its legs, to swoop and glide as it hunted insects in the forests of the late Triassic period.

An "eggcellent" idea
The reptilian egg was a safe, nutritious place for the embryo (unborn baby) to grow. It allowed reptiles to roam freely and spread their species over large areas, unlike amphibians, which had to lay their eggs in water.

*Coelophysis
(230 mya)*

Triassic murder mystery
Early reptiles dominated the land until about 250 million years ago. Then many suddenly died out, for reasons that are still unknown.

Twenty million years later, their former habitats were filled by the first dinosaurs, such as the small, meat-eating Coelophysis (left). Had the dinosaurs just taken over after a great disaster? Or did they outcompete the early reptiles?

Tiny mysteries
500 million years ago, many new life forms were appearing. Hallucigenia was one of the oddest. A caterpillarlike creature with 14 legs and spines on its back (above), no one really knows what it was.

The Early MYSTERIES

Bones of dinosaurs and other large animals were first described by scientists in the 1600s, but even the Romans had dug up such remains. These probably inspired legends. Elephant skulls, which have an opening in the middle of the head, almost certainly inspired the one-eyed Cyclops featured in the ancient Greek poem *The Odyssey*, and for centuries, people believed that large fossils were the remains of animals drowned in the biblical flood.

DINO-WARS
In the late 19th century, a "war" broke out between two American paleontologists, Othniel Marsh and Edward Drinker Cope. Each wanted to collect, name, and describe more dinosaurs than the other. This fight led to many major discoveries, which now fill museums throughout the country.

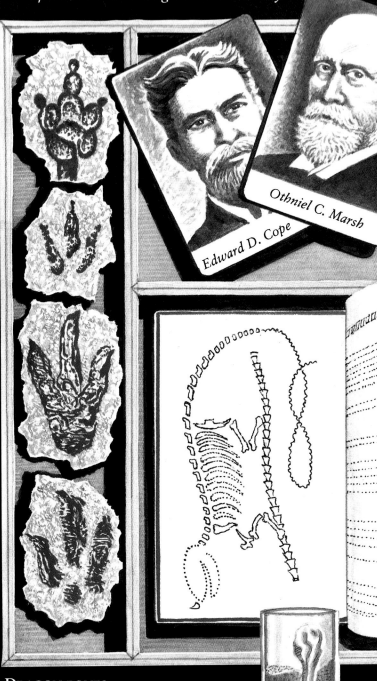

Edward D. Cope

Othniel C. Marsh

GIANT PRINTS
In 1835, Edward Hitchcock described some giant footprints found in Massachusetts. Some people believed they had been left by Noah's raven, but Hitchcock said they had come from huge birds. Only after his death were they recognized as dinosaur tracks.

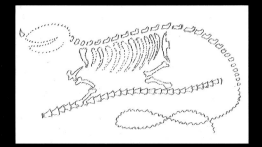

"MANTELL" PIECE *Gideon Mantell, an English doctor, was one of the first people to identify dinosaur bones. He realized they belonged to giant reptiles. He reconstructed a dinosaur (above) and named it* Iguanodon.

DRAGON BONES
In some parts of China, dinosaur bones are still thought to be the remains of dragons and are ground up for medicinal purposes.

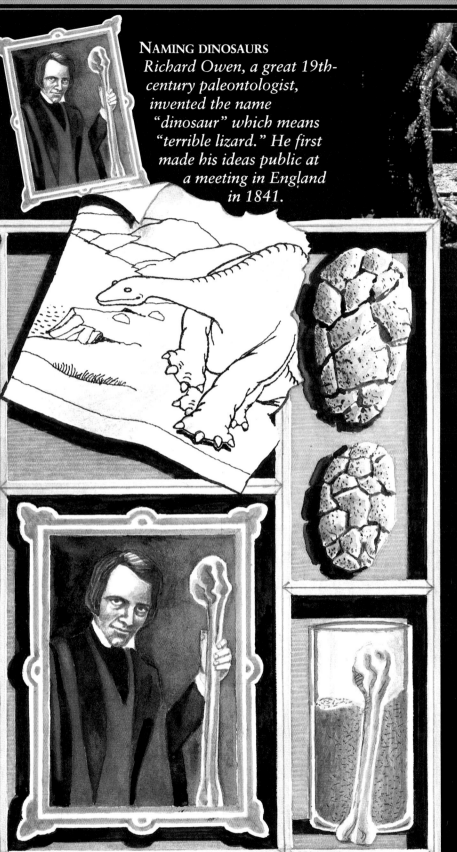

NAMING DINOSAURS
Richard Owen, a great 19th-century paleontologist, invented the name "dinosaur" which means "terrible lizard." He first made his ideas public at a meeting in England in 1841.

DINOSAURS AT THE MOVIES
Dinosaurs have appeared in many films, from King Kong *to* Jurassic Park *(above). The first dinosaur film was made in 1912 and starred a friendly sauropod called Gertie (above right).*

NESTING DINOSAURS
An expedition to Mongolia made one of the first discoveries of dinosaur eggs, in 1923. A dinosaur found with them was thought to have been an egg thief, but new findings show that it was the parent sitting on the nest (see page 146).

Dinosaurs at the Palace
The first model dinosaurs were displayed at Crystal Palace, London, in 1853. They look strange now, but they amazed everyone at the time!

Who first wrote about dinosaur bones? The first description of a dinosaur bone was published by Robert Plot in England, in 1676. He thought it was part of a giant human. The bone is now lost.

> *"I saw the back of the skull and it was a dinosaur...Here was THE fossil. And I just let out the biggest yell...YAHHHHHHHH! WE FOUND IT!"*
>
> Paul Sereno, on discovering *Eoraptor*, 1994

Investigations and
THEORIES

The study of dinosaurs begins with discovery and collection. Many of the best fossils come from remote parts of the world, such as the Gobi Desert of Mongolia, the Badlands of North Dakota, and even Antarctica.

Collection is a long, difficult, and delicate process. Each bone must be uncovered, dug out, and encased in plaster to prevent any damage during transportation. In the laboratory, the bones are prepared and cleaned with toothbrushes, dental picks, and tiny drills. The best-preserved skeletons are mounted for display in museums, supported by a steel frame or hung by fine wires from the ceiling. Scientists carefully measure, draw, photograph, and describe each bone.

This kind of research is the beginning of all our ideas and theories about dinosaurs. The rocks that contain fragments of dinosaurs, and other fossil animals and plants tell us much about dinosaurs and the world in which they lived.

Daily Life of a DINOSAUR

Fossils reveal a great deal about the dinosaurs. Skeletons indicate their size and shape, while their teeth and dung show how and what they ate. The shapes of their limbs and their tracks tell us how they moved. Their skeletons may reveal the age at which they died and whether they had diseases. Blowing into models of their noses can even reproduce the sounds they made. But many mysteries remain. We do not know their body temperature or color, the number of species, or why they died out.

Prehistoric snacks

Dinosaur teeth can reveal much about their diets. Hadrosaurs had sets of teeth (right) to grind conifer needles. Bones, seeds, or leaves found in fossils also show what different dinosaurs ate.

GIANT DINOSAURS

Sauropods such as Brachiosaurus *were the largest land animals.* Seismosaurus, *found recently in North America, was up to 164 ft (50 m) long and 100 tons in weight.*

CLEVER CREATURES

Most dinosaurs had small brains (like this Tyrannosaurus *brain, right) and were as intelligent as reptiles. But some hunters had larger brains and may have been as clever as their descendants, the birds.*

PACK ATTACK

Some meat-eating dinosaurs, such as Deinonychus *(right), may have hunted in groups so they could catch large prey. Packs of* Deinonychus *were far more dangerous than a single* Tyrannosaurus.

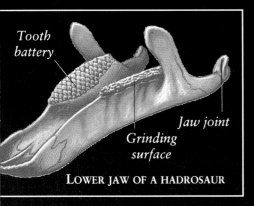

Tooth battery

Jaw joint

Grinding surface

LOWER JAW OF A HADROSAUR

ANCIENT FOOTPRINTS

There are hundreds of dinosaur tracks in ancient sand and mud flats. They show that small dinosaurs could run quickly and that many dinosaurs, even huge sauropods, moved in herds.

LAYING HABITS

All dinosaurs probably laid eggs. Most were oval-shaped and ranged from 6 inches (15 cm) wide to the size of soccer balls. Groups of eggs were usually arranged in circles, but some have been found in spiral shapes or lines. No one knows why the dinosaurs did this.

What is a species?
A species is the basic unit of classification. The members of a species have the same characteristics and differ from all other creatures. Similar species are grouped together in a genus.

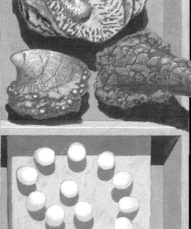

OUTWITTING THE ENEMY
Plant-eating dinosaurs had to protect themselves from the meat-eaters. Stegosaurs (above) covered themselves with spikes and spines, while the ankylosaurs (below) had a layer of "armor" and a swinging club tail.

SCARY BUT SLUGGISH
Tyrannosaurus rex *weighed 10 tons and could only reach a speed of about 21 miles (35 km) per hour. It was too heavy to be agile; if it fell while running it could be injured or killed. A human would be able to outrun it.*

DINOSAUR NAMES
Each dinosaur name is composed of 2 words: the genus (group of species), then the species. The name tells us about the animal. Velociraptor mongoliensis (left), for example, means "speedy hunter from Mongolia."

Still to SOLVE

HOW MANY DINOSAURS?
Paleontologists have found about 1,000 species of dinosaurs – a tiny fraction of all the species that ever lived. Each species was represented by millions of individuals, so, even if only one in a million dinosaurs was fossilized, thousands must still remain to be discovered and named.

More scientists than ever before are studying dinosaurs. More dinosaurs have been found in the last twenty years than over the previous 200 years. But there is much we do not know about these amazing creatures. No living animals are anything like dinosaurs, so we can only get information from fossils. Recently, there have been some important discoveries: nesting grounds, fossilized skin, a dinosaur on its nest, and several new species. Scientists are also learning more about the animals and plants that lived with the dinosaurs.

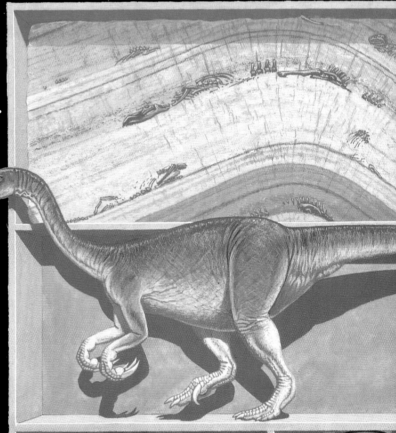

DINOSAUR IN THE DOCK
In 1992, the FBI "arrested" "Sue" the Tyrannosaurus rex, *which was at the center of a legal battle over its ownership. Nobody knows when Sue will get out of jail!*

A VERY ODD DINOSAUR
Among the peculiar dinosaurs found in the Gobi Desert of Mongolia, segnosaurs (left) are the strangest. They have a toothless beak, long neck, deep body, huge claws, and short legs. Their origins are unknown. New fossils have been found recently, so they may not be a mystery for long.

Were dinosaurs hot-blooded or cold-blooded?
At first, dinosaurs were thought to have been cold-blooded. In 1967, the idea of hot-blooded dinosaurs was proposed, based on their posture, bones, and diet. But most scientists disagree. They think dinosaurs had cold or lukewarm blood. New studies of their breathing systems suggest they are right.

DINOSAURS OF TODAY
Sir Arthur Conan Doyle's The Lost World *(right) was one of the first books to suggest that dinosaurs might still exist. Many people claim to have seen living sauropods in Africa, but no expedition has ever found them.*

CANNIBAL COELOPHYSIS
A recently discovered skeleton of Coelophysis *(see page 121) was found to contain the remains of another* Coelophysis *inside its rib cage. The animal on the inside is too large to be an unborn baby...so it is believed to have been the last meal of the larger dinosaur.*

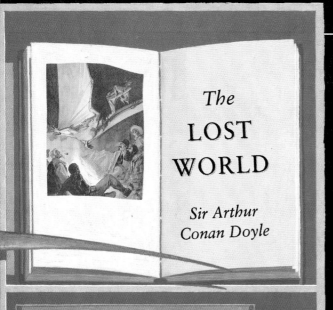

The
LOST WORLD

Sir Arthur Conan Doyle

Brachiosaurus

The death of the dinosaurs
"Why did the dinosaurs become extinct?" is the question that paleontologists are asked most often. One dinosaur expert once counted more than 100 theories of dinosaur extinction! But it is still not known which of these, if any, is true. Perhaps there was a global catastrophe, such as a meteorite hitting the Earth (below), or perhaps it was something more simple, such as volcanic eruptions or changes in the climate. Some scientists argue that the dinosaurs did not really die out, because their descendants, the birds, still exist today.

IMPOSSIBLE SAUROPODS
Sauropods like Brachiosaurus *(right and above) ate the equivalent of 50 bales of hay every day. How did all this food manage to pass through such a tiny head?*

"*We are awestruck by* Tyranosaurus; *we marvel at the feathers of* Archeopterix…*But none of these has taught us anywhere near so much…as a little 2-inch Cambrian odd-ball invertebrate named* Opabinia"

Steven Jay Gould, 1990

The Diversity OF LIFE

Fossils reveal a "grand procession of life" stretching far back into the early part of the Earth's history. Large chunks of this history were dominated by particular kinds of organisms.

The Mesozoic era, for example, is often called the "Age of Dinosaurs" and the Cenozoic, which followed it, is known as the "Age of Mammals." These "Ages" did not blend smoothly into each other. Instead, they often ended with global catastrophes that swept away entire groups of animals. An event at the end of the Permian Period, 250 million years ago, killed over 95 percent of all life on Earth.

What causes these events and what actually happens while they are taking place are two of the most important questions that science has yet to answer. But these mass extinctions were not all bad. They allowed new kinds of life to appear and form new groups. Without these events, the "Age of Dinosaurs" would still be going on, and humans would not exist.

Mesozoic CHANGES

The world's last dinosaurs lived alongside many other animals and plants. Some of these organisms are still with us today, but most became extinct at the same time as the dinosaurs. The Mesozoic world was much warmer than our own and supported a rich variety of life. Instead of whales and dolphins, the seas were filled with plesiosaurs and ichthyosaurs, and the dinosaurs ruled on the land. Mammals scurried around beneath their feet while their smaller reptilian cousins – turtles, lizards, and crocodiles – lived much as they do today. The air teemed with pterosaurs and the first birds – small, feathered dinosaurs – which fluttered from treetop to treetop.

DRAGONS OF THE SKIES
Fish-eating pterosaurs flew long before birds. Most were the size of crows, but some became enormous, with 40-ft (12-m) wingspans – the size of small fighter planes.

Pterosaur ("winged lizard")

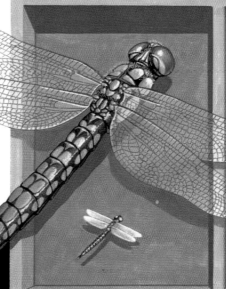

Was the atmosphere different in the Mesozoic era?
Some scientists argue that the amounts of gases making up the atmosphere may have been different in the Dinosaur Age. They claim that there was more oxygen, which enabled the dinosaurs to reach giant sizes and huge pterosaurs to fly through the air. But evidence, such as tiny bubbles of prehistoric air trapped in amber, is difficult to gather and much work remains to be done.

FURRY...AND SCARED!
Mammals hid from the dinosaurs by staying small and only emerging at night. Almost all we know about them is based on their teeth, which best survived fossilization.

THE DEADLY MESOZOIC SEAS

Plesiosaurs were the fiercest marine creatures. The long-necked types ate fish, but those with short necks and vast jaws (over 6 feet (2 m) long) ate meat. Bones with bite marks show that they even ate each other.

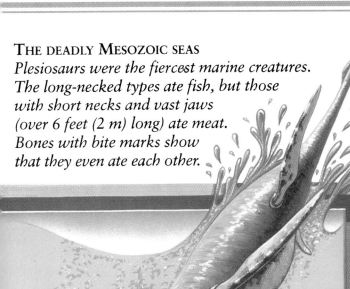

THE MOST SUCCESSFUL CREATURES

Insects were one of the first groups to colonize the land. In good conditions, huge forms appeared, such as dragonflies with wingspans of up to 2 feet (0.5 m). Most types of insects had evolved by the Mesozoic era, so the dinosaurs must have been pestered by flies, mosquitoes, and perhaps even fleas.

The dinosaur world

During the Mesozoic era, there were no polar ice caps and the continents were in different positions than where they are today. Previously, all the land had been joined together in one giant "supercontinent," known as Pangaea. This was now breaking into two parts – Laurasia in the north and Gondwanaland in the south. The world's climate was very mild, with warm conditions extending almost as far as the Arctic.

Laurasia

Gondwanaland

DINO FODDER

Early Mesozoic plants, upon which herbivorous (plant-eating) dinosaurs grazed, were mostly ferns, conifers, cycads, ginkgoes (left), and horsetails. Flowering plants first appeared about 100 million years ago, providing the last dinosaurs with a new diet.

Mesozoic plant and insect fossils

Early
MAMMALS

EARLY DUMBOS
The first elephants were tuskless and pig-sized. Mammoths, mastodons, and modern elephants all descended from them.

HUNGRY HORSES
50-million-year-old horses from Germany still have remains of skin and hair, and of leaves in their stomachs.

A mass extinction at the end of the Mesozoic era wiped out the dinosaurs and other groups. Mammals now had a chance to flourish and many new kinds appeared. Some were very successful and their descendants – whales, tigers, bats, humans, and hedgehogs – still exist. Many species had vanished by the end of the last Ice Age, but the reason is unclear. Was it climate changes... or hungry humans?

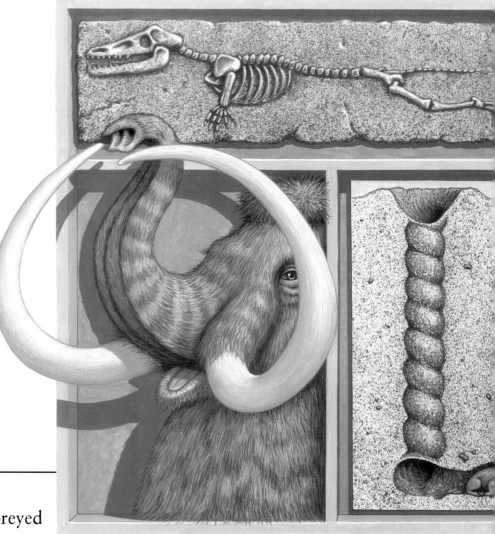

Horse-eating birds

Early mammals were preyed upon by huge, flightless birds, the phororhacids. These creatures often grew up to 10 ft (3 m) tall. With their powerful beaks, they could catch, kill, and tear apart land animals such as the first horses, which were only about the same size as modern-day sheep.

TWIST AND TURN
In 1976, mysterious, corkscrew-shaped holes were found in rocks in Nebraska (above). The fossilized remains of prehistoric beavers at the bottom of the holes gave scientists the answer – they were early burrows.

The "Giraffe-Rhinoceros"
Weighing 30 tons, and standing taller than 16 ft (5.5 m) at the shoulder, Indricotherium was the largest land mammal of all time. It lived in Asia and probably fed on the tops of small trees.

Living Tanks
Glyptodons were the strangest mammals that ever lived. The ancestors of armadillos, these animals, which were up to 12 ft (3.5 m) long, had bony body armor including an armored tail.

Sea Legs
The recent fossil discovery of Ambulocetus *shows that these ancestors of whales had four legs and lived on land. They returned to the water over 50 million years ago.*

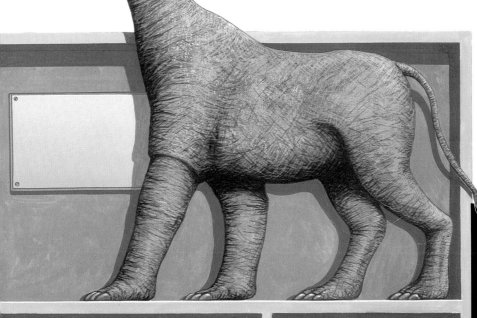

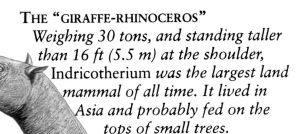

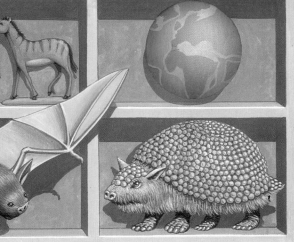

What is a mammal?
Living mammals are distinguished by their hair and mammary glands (from which they get their name), but these are rarely found in fossils. Luckily, mammal teeth have a distinctive shape and are often the only parts to be preserved. Mammals also have an unusual jaw joint. Fossils clearly show the evolution of this feature over time.

Going Batty
Bats first appeared 50 million years ago. Icaronycteris, the oldest known bat (above), was not very different from modern bats. Later fossils show that early bats could echolocate (navigate using sound waves).

Marsupial Mystery
Marsupials (animals that rear their young in pouches) are found only in Australasia and South America. When Pangaea split, their ancestors were carried on these continents.

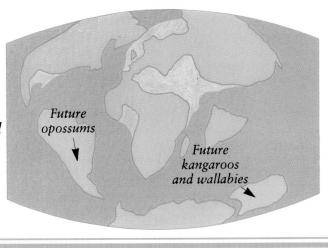

Future opossums

Future kangaroos and wallabies

"Our reverence for the nobility of manhood will not be lessened by the knowledge that Man is, in substance and in structure, on with the brutes."

T.H. Huxley, *Man's Place in Nature*, 1863

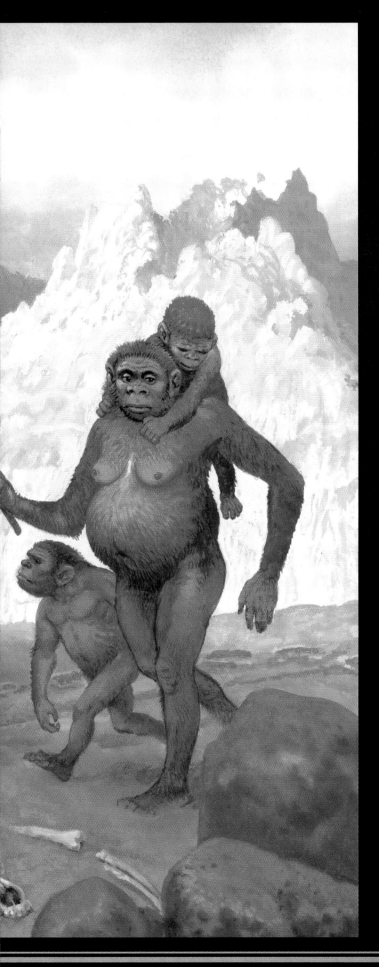

The Emergence OF HUMANS

We humans are fascinated by our own ancestry. Each new discovery, even if it is only half a tooth, is greeted as a sensation. Many scientists are expending much time and a great deal of effort in the search for our ancestors, but they face a huge problem.

Our family, the hominids, has left few fossils. Most of the remains found consist of odd teeth, bones, or just fragments. Skulls are important, but they are also rare, and all the skeletons that have been found are incomplete.

With so little evidence, scientists can only guess at our origins, and arguments are common. Fortunately, major fossil findings are still being made. Work in Ethiopia has uncovered our earliest known ancestors. Over four million years old, the fossils are from a small, apelike creature which probably lived mainly in woodlands. Its teeth are similar to those of the chimpanzee and show that the human line may be more closely related to chimps than to any other living apes.

Missing Links and EARLY THEORIES

NEANDERTHAL MYTHS
Early reconstructions of Neanderthals were cartoonlike with exaggerated features (below) and stooped poses (left). New studies suggest they were much like us.

Until the mid-19th century, Christians believed that humans had been created by God. Darwin (see page 121) and his supporters argued that we had descended from earlier, apelike forms and that we were simply part of the animal kingdom. This caused much anger and the "Darwinians" were ridiculed. But most people gradually accepted the idea, and the search to find our ancestors began.

At first, scientists thought that the development of humans would be a simple line of species, each of which looked a little more like us. But modern studies show that our history is complex and we have a long way to go before we unravel all the details.

THE QUEST FOR THE "MISSING LINK"

19th-century scientists wanted to find a single "missing link" between people and apes. Dutch paleontologist Eugène Dubois thought he had found it when he discovered bones in Java in 1891. In fact, they were the remains of Homo erectus.

CONTROVERSY AND HATRED

Outrage against Darwin reached its peak in 1871, when he published The Descent of Man. *This upheld his theory that humans were part of the animal world and close to apes. Cartoons appeared ridiculing his ideas (left) and he was accused of denying Christian teachings.*

THE GIANT APES
Ten-million-year-old fossils of apes, found in Asia, were once thought to be our ancestors. Some were up to 8 feet (2.5 m) tall. In fact, they are probably related to orangutans.

TAUNG CHILD
In 1925, Raymond Dart announced the discovery of an infant man-ape in the Transvaal, South Africa. The scientific community attacked Dart, saying that he had found the remains of a chimpanzee or gorilla. But further discoveries showed that he was right. He had found evidence of our ancestor Australopithecus (see page 140), which lived over three million years ago.

"Taung Child"
(*Australopithecus*)

Out of Africa
When fossil humans were found in the 1800s, it was thought that humans originated in Asia. But early this century, Africa started to yield fossils. Finds like this skull from Kenya show that human origins must lie in Africa.

Who was "Piltdown man?"
In 1912, a strange skull was found at Piltdown, England. Was this a "missing link?" In 1952, it was shown to be a hoax – a human skull and an ape's jaw. The hoaxer's identity is still a mystery.

THE GREAT DEBATE
A new problem has divided researchers. Richard Leakey (far right) argues that the direct line leading to humans is very old; Donald Johanson (right) claims that our species split from other hominids quite recently. There is not yet enough evidence to prove either theory.

The Origin
OF HUMANS

Our species, *Homo sapiens* is grouped with other (extinct) species in the genus *Homo*. This and the genus *Australopithecus* make up the family *Hominidae (hominids)*. Many other genera and species have been named, but recent fossil discoveries show that few of these, if any, are real. To understand our past more fully, we must investigate the biology, habits, and history of our extinct hominid relatives.

Well-traveled hominids
Our nearest relative, *Homo erectus*, was still living 200,000 years ago, alongside the first members of our own species. *Homo erectus* looked a lot like us,

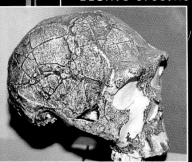

but had heavy eyebrow ridges, a heavy jaw, and no defined chin. Tall, narrow-hipped, and long-legged, *Homo erectus* was able to travel over long distances. The species spread from Africa to Europe, Siberia, Java, and China about a million years ago.

MONKEY BUSINESS
Primates (monkeys and apes) are characterized by their big brains, opposable thumbs, nails instead of claws, and care of their young. Our closest relatives are African apes which include the chimpanzee, gorilla, and orangutan.

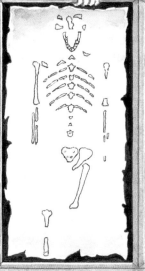

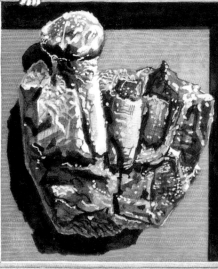

THE "SOUTHERN APE"
Three million years ago, an apelike creature, 3-4.5 ft (1-1.5 m) high, ran upright across the African plains. Australopithecus, our ancestor, had come down from the trees to eat. Large, thick teeth helped it to grind its food, which mainly consisted of fruit and leaves. But the ground was dangerous – hyenas and leopards were constantly looking for prey.

"HANDY HUMAN"

Homo habilis, *from Africa, was the first to use simple tools. Fossils and tools are often found on the edges of ancient lakes and rivers – good sites to catch prey as they came to drink.*

I LOVE LUCY

In 1975, a stunning discovery was made in Hadar, Ethiopia. Bones from a family group of at least thirteen individuals of Australopithecus were found in sediments beside a lake. The most complete specimen, a young female, was nicknamed Lucy. She showed that Australopithecus had a primitive skull on top of a modern body.

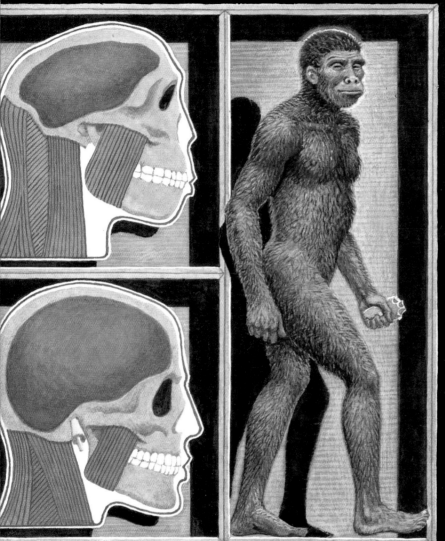

HUMANS STAND UP

Nearly four million years ago, two of our ancestors walked upright across ash deposited at Laetoli, Tanzania, by a recent volcanic eruption nearby. Their footprints were preserved in the ash and can still be seen there today. The prints show that, even at this very early stage of their evolution, humans stood upright and walked in the same way as modern humans, with long, swinging strides.

How old is our species? The earliest definite remains of Homo sapiens are about 120,000 years old. But the Petralona skull from Greece, dated at 300-400,000 years old, is claimed by some to belong to our species, and genetic studies also suggest that we have been around for at least 200-300,000 years.

BIG BRAINS

Homo sapiens *(right) have larger (0.2642-gallons) brains than* Homo erectus *(left). The first big-brained ancestor was* Homo habilis *("handy man"). Their tools suggest they were left- or right-handed, so they had "lopsided" brains like us. Skulls show that the speech areas of the brain were developed, but we will never know how they spoke.*

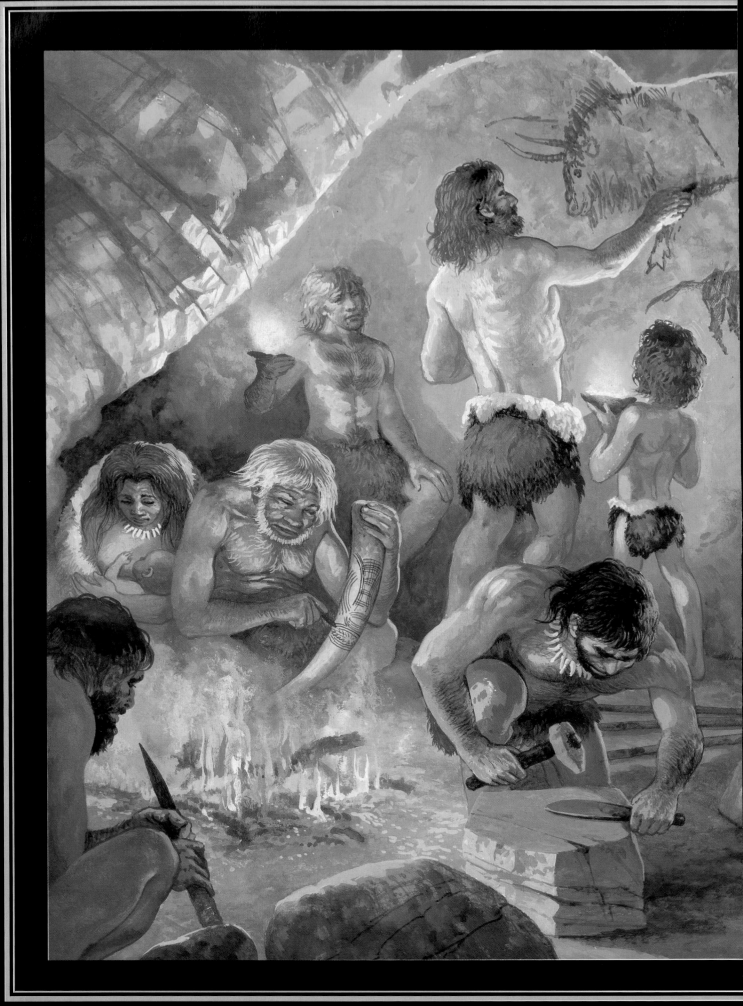

> "The fossil hunter does not kill; he resurrects. And the result of his sport is to add to the...treasures of human knowledge."
>
> George Gaylord Simpson, *Attending Marvels*, 1934

Discoveries and TECHNOLOGY

In terms of life on Earth, modern humans are the most advanced species – but not the last! We are newcomers, having only been around for a few hundreds of thousands of years.

You might think that because of this, there should be a lot of evidence for our history, but this is not the case. Speech, behavior, and social customs do not fossilize and we can only guess at them from indirect evidence like skeleton structure and tool design.

The biggest problem is the origin of our own species, *Homo sapiens*. Some scientists think that we originated in Africa about 200,000 years ago; others say that we are descended from *Homo erectus* (see page 140).

Today, genetic studies of people around the world are providing new answers to this debate. One study suggests that modern humans are descended from a single female who lived in Africa between 150,000 and 300,000 years ago. Could this incredible claim be true?

Examining our ANCESTORS

MAMMOTH KILLERS
Mammoths and other large animals vanished from North America about 12,000 years ago. Had they been hunted and butchered to extinction by groups of early humans?

The early history of our species saw many innovations: the development of speech and language; the evolution of complex social groups; the beginnings of thought; and the appearance of religion with systems of beliefs and ceremonies. There were also many important technological innovations: the taming of fire; the invention of new materials and methods for producing clothes; shelters; and more complex, effective tools. We do not know exactly how, when, or even why many of these innovations came about, but there are hundreds of theories – and hundreds of scientists willing to test them out.

THE ICE AGE WORLD
(2,000,000 – 11,000 years ago)

The Ice Age
Much of *Homo sapiens'* history took place during the Ice Age. In the coldest phases, glaciers spread and the sea level fell, while in the warm periods, climates were hotter than today. Such events probably caused changes in our evolution.

A KEY TO THE PAST

Just a shin bone and a tooth tell us a lot about Boxgrove man. Patterns on the tooth show that he ate raw vegetables as well as meat...and suffered from toothaches!

What happened to the Neanderthals? About 30,000 years ago, the Neanderthals suddenly vanished. No one knows if they were wiped out naturally or by their relative Homo sapiens.

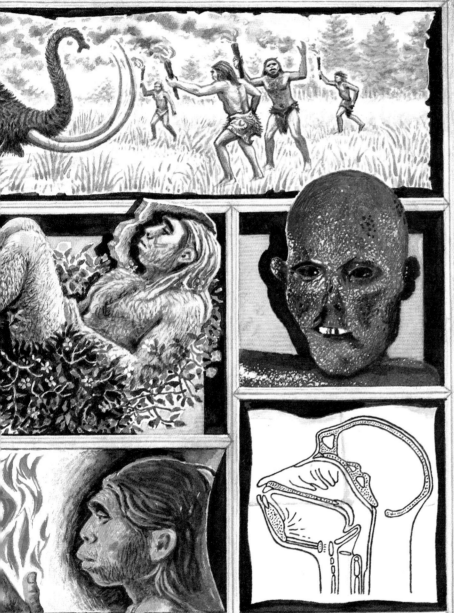

ARTY HUMANS
Art was important to the Cro-Magnons, the earliest Homo sapiens. Their best-known works are cave paintings. Other art forms included sculptures in bone, ivory, or clay, engravings, and jewelry.

FUNERAL CUSTOMS
Neanderthals seem to have been the first to bury their dead, often with tools, bones, and flowers. Many graves contain old or diseased bodies; Neanderthals must have cared for the elderly and the sick.

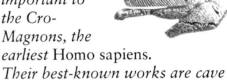

TOOLS OF THE TRADE
Cro-Magnons made sophisticated tools like spearheads (above), needles, blades, and even flutes. Flint was used at first; bone, antler, and other materials came later.

THE TALKING APE
Our brain's speech areas are over two million years old. Throats able to shape words appeared one million years later, reaching today's form 300,000 years ago.

FIRE!
Humans had begun to use fire over half a million years ago. They now had protection, a source of heat, and a way of making food easier to eat.

THE MYSTERIOUS ICEMAN
In 1991, the mummified body of a 5,000-year-old Neolithic man was found in a glacier. "Ötzi," complete with his tools and clothes, has solved many secrets of Neolithic life.

The Latest
INVESTIGATIONS

Modern technology has enabled paleontologists to make enormous progress in the last ten years. New dating techniques, computers, scanners, X ray machines, scanning electron microscopes, and satellites have all provided new ways of searching for, collecting, and analyzing fossils. Paleontologists have also been helped by other areas of science, such as studies of genes which contain a record of the past.

How can we tell the age of fossils?
There are two basic ways of dating fossils: Radioactive decay, based on the fact that some elements emit radiation and change their nature over time; and fossils themselves, which are typical of certain prehistoric eras.

GENE GENIUS
Scientists are now able to study our genes (the materials that give us our characteristics). Most studies have tried to discover which living ape is our closest relative; they tend to agree that it is the chimpanzee. On rare occasions, genes are preserved in fossils. If early human genetic material is ever found, it may lead to some surprising new ideas.

NESTING DINOSAURS
New discoveries are being made faster than ever, due to better excavation techniques. In 1994, an expedition to Mongolia found a dinosaur, Oviraptor, *preserved sitting on a nest full of eggs (above). Previous finds had suggested that this dinosaur was a nest-raider (its name means "egg-stealer"). We now know that it was a good parent, guarding its nest even to the point of death.*

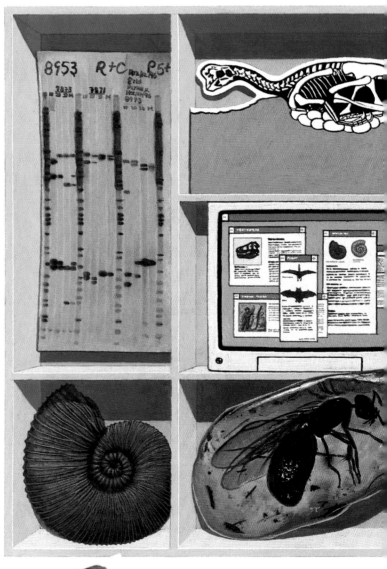

ART GALLERY FROM THE PAST
The last decade has unearthed many cave paintings. Those in Grotte Chauvet, France include the only known images of a leopard, rhinoceros, and panther. Footprints had been left by the last viewer, 30,000 years ago.

146

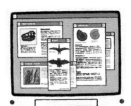

Computers are rapidly becoming the scientist's most important tool. They can analyze large volumes of data and help to record the positions of findings. In the future, they will be used to produce and compare images.

FOSSIL CARE
Preparing fossils for study or display is a difficult task. Simple tools like drills, knives, and needles are used. Other equipment includes acid baths to dissolve rock around the fossil, and high-pressure air to blast off any sediment.

FACT OR FICTION?
Films and books about prehistoric life have highlighted important scientific questions. For example, could dinosaur genes be reconstructed from blood preserved in fossilized mosquitos, as suggested in Jurassic Park?

The unsolved mysteries

The science of paleontology is only a little over two hundred years old. There is so much left to discover and so many mysteries to solve that it will be hundreds or thousands of years, before scientists have even begun to exhaust all the possibilities of their research.

But paleontology does not always require expensive machines and the latest technology. Every day, amateurs all around the world collect fossils – and some of them turn out to be important pieces of the puzzle that is the "tree of life." You could go hunting for fossils tomorrow and make such a major discovery. You might even solve one of the great mysteries of the prehistoric world.

ELECTRONIC EYES

For years, paleontologists used ordinary microscopes to study fossils. Today, electronic machines allow them to see much further. The electron microscope can identify the finest structures (above). Scanners can build images of the outside and inside of skulls, providing information which would be otherwise inaccessible.

4.6 BYA-597 MYA
PRECAMBRIAN ERA
3.5 bya First life appears
640 mya Multicelled
organisms known to exist

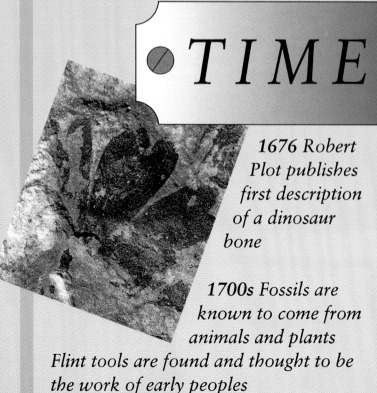

1676 Robert
Plot publishes
first description
of a dinosaur
bone

597-250 MYA PALEOZOIC ERA
570-505 mya Cambrian period
505-438 mya Ordovician period
438-408 mya Silurian period
408-360 mya Devonian period;
fish and amphibians appear
360-286 mya Carboniferous period;
amphibians dominate
286-250 mya Permian period;
reptiles dominate

1700s Fossils are
known to come from
animals and plants
Flint tools are found and thought to be
the work of early peoples

250-65 MYA MESOZOIC ERA
250-208 mya Triassic period; dinosaurs emerge
208-144 mya Jurassic period; giant dinosaurs evolve
144-65 mya Cretaceous period; flowers and insects appear
65 mya Dinosaurs are wiped out by an unknown cause

65 MYA-PRESENT CENOZOIC ERA
50 mya Monkeys
30 mya Apes
3.5-2 mya
Australopithecus
2-1.5 mya
Homo habilis
**1.5 mya-200,000
ya** Homo erectus
**200,000-35,000
ya** Homo
neanderthalensis
200,000 ya-today
Homo sapiens

1824 Megalosaurus *is
first dinosaur to be
named scientifically*
1825 Gideon Mantell
draws Iguanodon
1841 Richard Owen
names dinosaurs
1853 First model
dinosaurs go on display
at Crystal Palace,
London, England

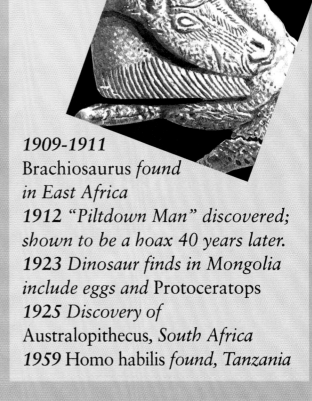

1856 Neanderthal fossil found, Germany

1858 First whole dinosaur fossil, Hadrosaurus, *discovered in North America*

1861 *Discovery of* Archaeopteryx *(the world's oldest bird)*

1865 *First discovery of Stone Age art, France*

1868 *Remains of Cro-Magnon humans discovered, France*

1909-1911 Brachiosaurus *found in East Africa*

1912 "Piltdown Man" *discovered; shown to be a hoax 40 years later.*

1923 Dinosaur finds in Mongolia include eggs and Protoceratops

1925 *Discovery of* Australopithecus, *South Africa*

1959 Homo habilis *found, Tanzania*

1871 Darwin publishes The Descent of Man

1878 *Herd of Iguanodon found, Belgium*

1879 *Stone Age cave paintings found, Spain*

1887 *Othniel C. Marsh discovers* Triceratops

1891 *Eugène Dubois discovers "Java Man"* (Homo erectus)

1902 Tyrannosaurus rex *discovered*

1906 *Neanderthal skeleton rebuilt wrongly, misdirecting ideas about early humans*

1963 *Studies show humans and chimps shared the same ancestor only five million years ago*

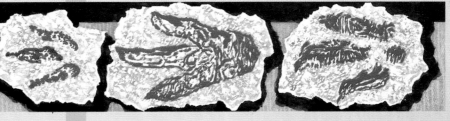

1975 "Lucy" found, Ethiopia

1983 Baryonyx *found, England*

1987 *First discovery of dinosaurs in Antarctica*

1991 "Ötzi" *found, Austria*

1994 Oviraptor *found nesting*

1995 Argentinosaurus *found – largest dinosaur ever*

1996 *Finds confirm* Carcharodontosaurus saharicus *(found 1927) as a match for* Tyrannosaurus rex

6. Cadbury Fort
7. Stonehenge
8. Corsica
9. Carthage
10. Alexandria
11. Amarna
12. Abu Simbel
13. Meroe
14. Nubia
15. Great
    Zimbabwe
16. Crete
17. Thera
18. Olympia
19. Mycenae
20. Anatolia
21. Troy
22. Palmyra
23. Qumran

1. Rock Eagle Mound
2. Tenochtitlan
3. Lake Guatavita
4. Nazca Lines
5. Macchu Picchu

24. Babylon
25. Edom
26. Dilmun
27. Bactria
28. Indus Valley
29. Altai tombs
30. Amazonian graves
31. Mount Li
32. Angkor
33. Easter Island

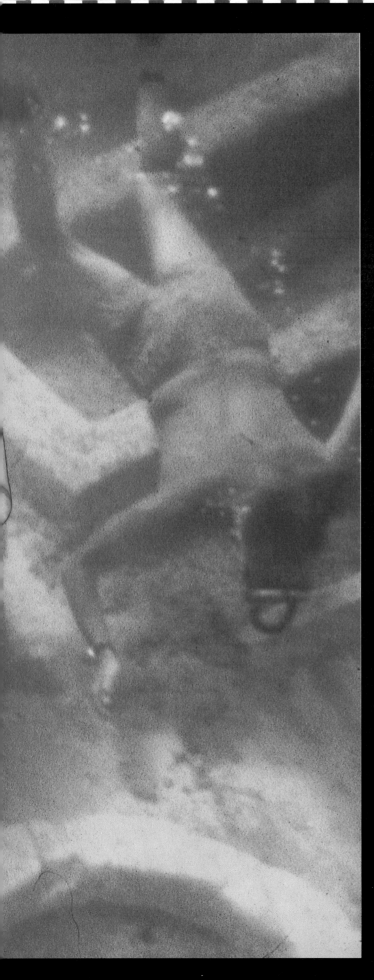

Chapter Five
LOST CIVILIZATIONS

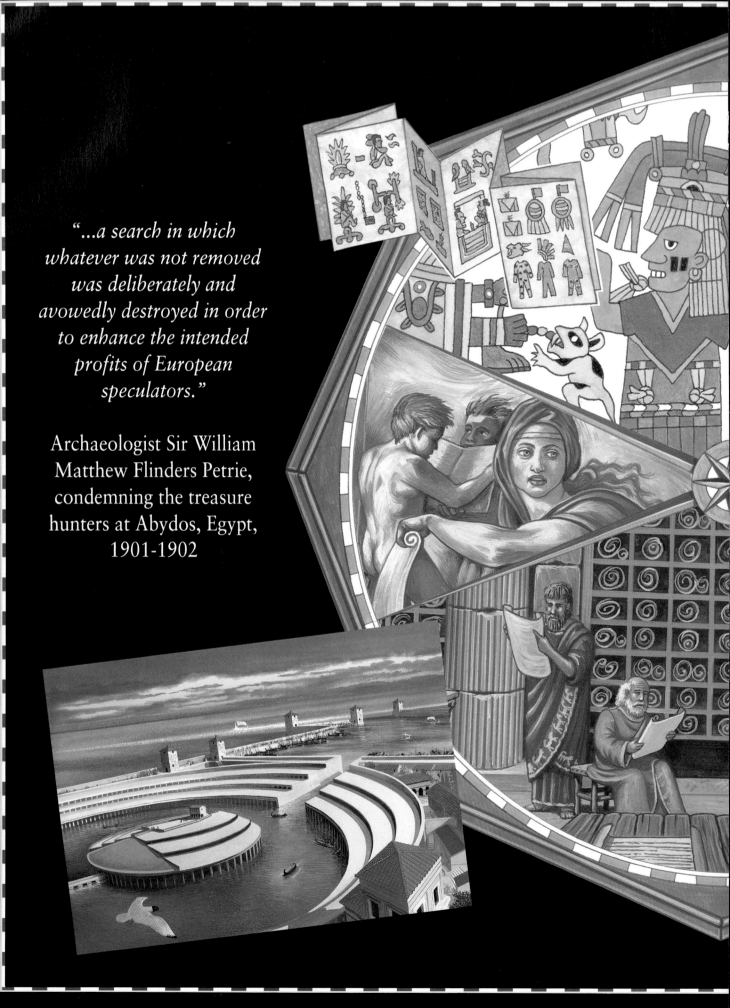

"...a search in which whatever was not removed was deliberately and avowedly destroyed in order to enhance the intended profits of European speculators."

Archaeologist Sir William Matthew Flinders Petrie, condemning the treasure hunters at Abydos, Egypt, 1901-1902

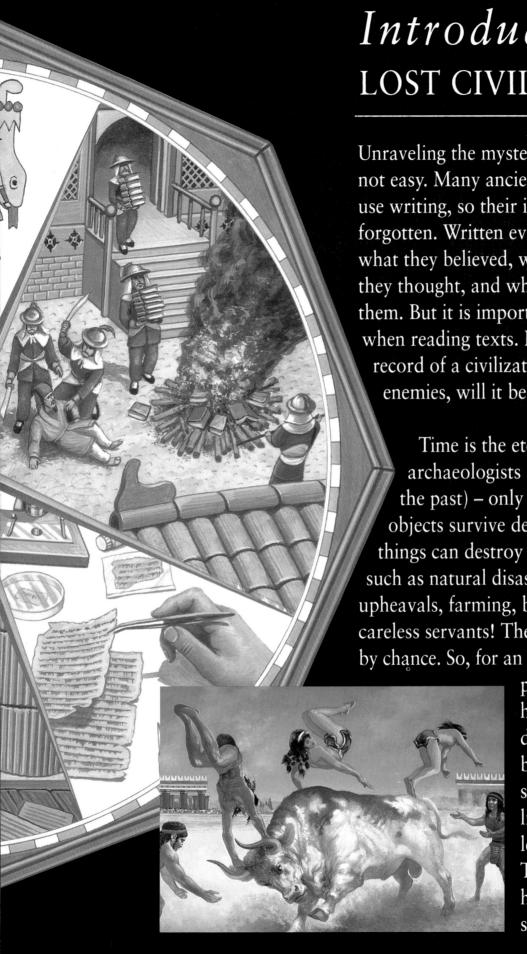

Introduction to
LOST CIVILIZATIONS

Unraveling the mysteries of the past is not easy. Many ancient peoples did not use writing, so their ideas and deeds are forgotten. Written evidence can tell us what they believed, what they did, what they thought, and what others thought of them. But it is important to be careful when reading texts. If the only surviving record of a civilization is written by its enemies, will it be a fair account?

Time is the eternal enemy of archaeologists (people who study the past) – only a few bodies and objects survive decay. Many other things can destroy clues to the past, such as natural disasters, wars, religious upheavals, farming, building – and even careless servants! They often survive only by chance. So, for an accurate view of the past, archaeologists have to turn into detectives, examining buildings and objects, studying texts, and listening to what legends tell them. They also need the help of all the latest scientific techniques.

Hidden PLACES

Some places are destroyed and disappear, almost without trace, until an archaeologist tracks down their remains. Sometimes a place is mentioned only in a much later text and is dismissed as a legend.

A good example is the siege of Troy (in modern-day Turkey), by the ancient Greeks. For centuries, the *Iliad* (700s B.C.), Homer's poem about the Trojan war, was regarded as fantasy. But an amateur archaeologist called Heinrich Schliemann passionately believed that it was true. In 1870, he began digging in the area where Homer had placed Troy – and found it! Excavations have proved that Homer knew many details about a civilization that had vanished centuries before he was born. Stories and songs had kept alive memories of such details as the city's defenses and the soldiers' armor. We cannot yet prove that the beautiful Helen of Troy existed, or what the wooden horse was (left), but we have learned not to simply dismiss the legends of the past.

"Was this the face that launch'd a thousand ships And burnt the topless towers of Ilium?"
Description of Helen of Troy in Christopher Marlowe's play *Doctor Faustus*, c. 1588

Lost and FOUND

Many buildings referred to in ancient writings are now totally destroyed, such as the Roman emperor Nero's fabulous Golden House. Sometimes we find ruins that can be identified beyond doubt, like Pompeii in Italy, which was buried by a volcanic eruption. But even if archaeologists can identify a site and have ancient texts describing it, they still have difficulty imagining what it was like at its peak. Ancient Greek writers said that the burial complex of King Amenemhet III of Egypt was one of the most magnificent buildings they had ever seen; now, only dreary piles of mud bricks are left! Only if we have a picture of such a place can we begin to imagine it in all its glory.

Can destruction ever have benefits? Sometimes it can reveal other treasures. During World War II, a bomb destroyed the ancient church of St. Bride's in London, England. This tragedy gave archaeologists a chance to excavate the site. They found earlier churches going back about 1,400 years and a Roman pavement from the second century A.D. St. Bride's was then rebuilt.

ROUND TABLE RIDDLES
In medieval legend, Camelot was the headquarters of King Arthur. If it existed, it was nothing like the fairy tale castles of Hollywood films! It may have been an old Celtic hill-fort, reoccupied by the English war-leader – a place of earth ramparts and wooden battlements. Archaeologists have found such a site at Cadbury Fort in England, which some people think might be Camelot.

GARDENS OF LEGEND
The Hanging Gardens of Babylon were built for a queen from the hill country, who was homesick for the plains of Babylonia. They were so completely destroyed that we cannot even identify the foundations. However, there are many theories on what they looked like (see page 37)!

ON THE TRAIL OF KING MINOS

In 1893, the archaeologist Sir Arthur Evans was shown some seal-stones covered in strange pictures. He tracked them to Crete, the legendary home of King Minos. Evans began to dig, and unearthed the mighty Minoan civilization. It had been ruined and forgotten – except in legend.

THE LIGHT OF THE MEDITERRANEAN

Built in about 280 B.C., the lighthouse of Alexandria, in Egypt, was 390 feet (117 m) high. Its beam could be seen for 30 miles (50 km). It was toppled by an earthquake in the 1300s, but we still have accounts and pictures of it. Pieces of it have been found in the harbor.

An Indian mystery

Excavations by Sir Robert Eric Mortimer Wheeler (1890-1976) revealed artifacts (below), seal-stones (left), and buildings of the Indus Valley civilization of ancient India. They invented their own writing system, but no one has managed to decipher it yet. Will we ever know who their rulers were, the purpose of their great ceremonial bath, or the identity of their god, the Lord of the Animals?

A GREAT TRIBUTE

In the fifth century B.C., the Greek sculptor Phidias made a great statue of the god Zeus to go in his temple at Olympia. It was 43 feet (13 m) tall and made of gold and ivory. In A.D. 393, a Roman emperor took it to Constantinople, but a fire swept the place where it was kept in A.D. 462, destroying it completely.

THE EFFECTS OF WAR

Conquerors often try to wipe out all traces of their enemies' culture. This was the fate of the Aztec and Inca peoples at the hands of 16th-century Spanish explorers. The great Aztec capital of Tenochtitlan was demolished. Its remains still lie under modern Mexico City.

157

The Stuff of LEGENDS

CONQUISTADORES!
The early Spanish conquerors of America were driven by a desire to serve God (by converting people to Christianity) and their king (by winning him an empire). But they were also ruthless and greedy, out to make their own fortunes from the gold of the "New World." In Colombia, they heard the fantastic but true story of El Dorado – the "Gilded Man" (see page 159).

When something really exciting happens, people like to tell the story over and over again. Unless it is written down immediately, it changes as time passes. Details get left out; others are added; the deeds of two or more people can be credited to one "super-hero." Over time, people even forget what some things were or what they meant, so they invent explanations – which are often wrong! A story might be given a new meaning so that it fits in with the politics and religion of the time. But somewhere, buried in every story, there remains a kernel of truth.

THE ULTIMATE QUEST
People have searched all over the world for Atlantis, but many now believe that the story was inspired by Minoan Crete. The memory of the great island kingdom with its powerful navy, the importance of bulls in its religion, and its sudden decline had become mixed up with natural disasters and myths. The stories were muddled and misunderstood as time passed, but some accounts do seem to contain an echo of the great Minoan civilization.

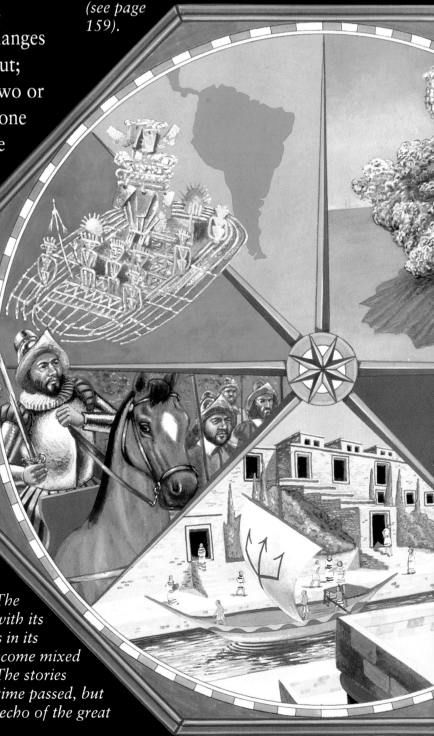

THE GOLDEN RULER
When a king came to the throne in the region of Lake Guatavita, Colombia, he was covered in gold dust then sailed to the middle of the lake, where he threw in gold offerings to the gods. Imagination and greed embroidered the story, and tales spread, of a city and a land made of gold. For two centuries, people searched for "El Dorado" and it cost many lives. Others tried to drain the lake, but failed.

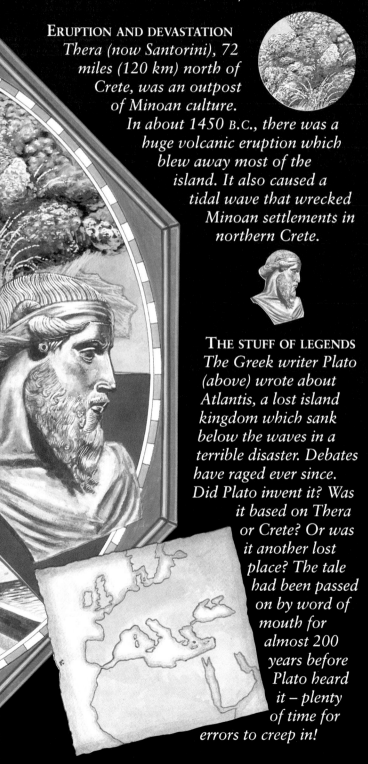

ERUPTION AND DEVASTATION
Thera (now Santorini), 72 miles (120 km) north of Crete, was an outpost of Minoan culture. In about 1450 B.C., there was a huge volcanic eruption which blew away most of the island. It also caused a tidal wave that wrecked Minoan settlements in northern Crete.

THE STUFF OF LEGENDS
The Greek writer Plato (above) wrote about Atlantis, a lost island kingdom which sank below the waves in a terrible disaster. Debates have raged ever since. Did Plato invent it? Was it based on Thera or Crete? Or was it another lost place? The tale had been passed on by word of mouth for almost 200 years before Plato heard it – plenty of time for errors to creep in!

King Solomon's mines
Some people have embarked on quests for things mentioned in the Bible – the Ark of the Covenant, the treasure from the temple of Jerusalem, Noah's Ark, and many others. Others have looked for places. The fabulous mines of King Solomon caught people's imagination and inspired films and novels. When the ruins of Great Zimbabwe (below) were found in Africa, some suggested that these were the famous mines. But Zimbabwe belongs to a much later African empire. Solomon's mines remain out of our grasp.

Can texts really lead us to lost places? Ancient Mesopotamian texts refer to a place called Dilmun, describing it as so wonderful that, until recently, scholars dismissed it as fantasy. Studies of earlier texts and ruins have shown that it was a staging post in the trade between Sumer and the Indus Valley. When the trade ceased, Dilmun was forgotten – in fact, it was the island of Bahrain!

The Lost CULTURES

All cultures change over time. We can follow the developments of long-lived civilizations, like those of ancient Egypt and China, over thousands of years. We can see how life has evolved in Europe since the fall of the Roman Empire in A.D. 476. People's ways of life have changed, but we can trace elements from the past to the present.

Even if a culture seems to have been wiped out, some things survive and are absorbed by a new civilization. Memories of lost cultures may live on in texts or in legends. Then one day, archaeologists may find solid remains.

Archaeologists often discover many surprises while exploring lost cultures. Some people still find it hard to accept that young Minoans (left) would leap through the horns of charging bulls – yet there are pictures and statues to prove it. Did they risk their lives in this way to please a god? Perhaps they believed that this god tossed their land with earthquakes as the bull tossed the athletes with its horns.

"...[the archaeologist] brings to light a mass of objects illustrating the arts and handicrafts of the past, the temples in which men worshiped, the houses in which they lived, the setting in which their lives were spent."

Sir Leonard Woolley, *Digging up the Past*, 1930

Decline, Destruction, AND DEATH

Some flourishing cultures have been quickly and totally destroyed, but this rarely happens so dramatically. Usually, many factors combine and there is a long, slow decline to extinction. Years of bad weather may cause famine, farmland can lose its fertility if over-used, and wood supplies run out if people cut down trees without replanting them. A vital river may change course or a harbor may silt up. Earthquakes, floods, and other natural disasters may occur. Trade may be disrupted or there may be wars and invasions. The people of a declining society may simply emigrate or decide to adopt the ways of more successful neighbors.

How do cultures become legends?
Through distortions of fact that happen over time. For example, one group of the Sea Peoples (see page 163) was called the Peleset. After their defeat by Egypt, they retreated and the land where they settled was named after them – Palestine. They appear in the Bible as the Philistines, the archenemies of the Hebrews.

OMENS OF DISASTER
A fiery comet in the early 1500s terrified the Aztecs of Central America. Was this a sign that their gods were angry with them? For ten years, many strange events occurred. The Aztecs thought they were doomed; they were – the Spaniards arrived (see page 158).

THE INCAS' LAST STAND
In 1911, the explorer Hiram Bingham set out for the Andes, armed with texts telling of cities where the last Incas had fought off the Spaniards. He found Machu Picchu, an Inca city that for 300 years had been hidden by the jungle.

THE MYSTERIOUS MYCENAEANS
After the decline of the Minoans, the Mycenaeans dominated trade in the Mediterranean Sea. They were rich and successful, but they declined too. By 1000 B.C., their civilization, artifacts (above), and writing system (right) had vanished. Only in legend did they and their heroes, such as Agamemnon, survive.

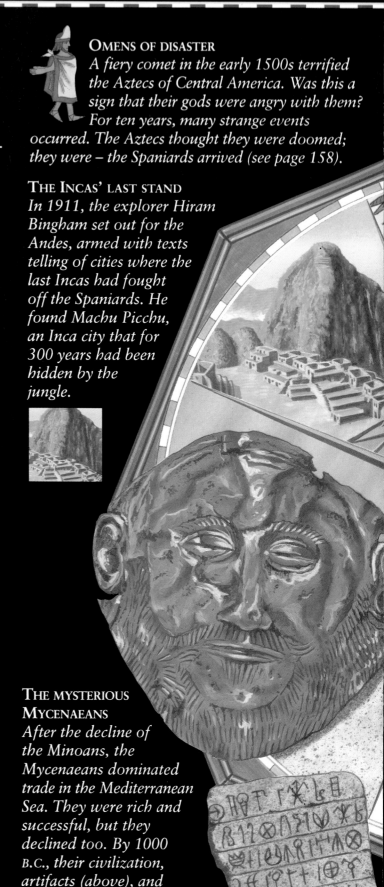

MYTHS OF THE MAYA

The Maya were once seen as a peace-loving people. But archaeologists have begun to decode their writing and it is clear that rival city-states fought constantly for power. Overfarming contributed to their decline, but so did these wars.

EGYPT

River Nile

Meroe

NUBIA

An advanced culture

The state of Meroe flourished from about 50 B.C. until about A.D. 350 and traded with Egypt, Africa, Greece, Rome, and India. Its culture was a blend of local customs and those of Egypt and other countries (such as pyramid tombs for its kings, below). Meroe's farmers grew cotton, brought from India. Its metalsmiths worked iron, and their methods spread into Africa. One text claims Meroe was so rich that its prisoners were held in golden chains! Attacks by other peoples led to its decline, but it collapsed after an invasion by the King of Axum in East Africa.

ATEN'S CITY

One king of Egypt, Akhenaton, believed that Aten was the only god. He built a new capital at Tel el Amarna and banned worship of other gods. But after his death, Amarna was left to the mercy of the desert sands.

INVADERS FROM THE SEA

Ancient Egyptian texts describe invasions by mysterious "Sea Peoples." These were from the declining Mycenaean empire, looking for new homes. In about 1190 B.C., they invaded what is now Turkey, wiping out the Hittites (see page 164). They were finally defeated by Ramses III, and scattered all over the Mediterranean.

Who Were THEY?

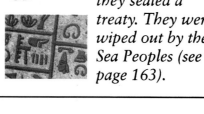

THE KEY TO A LOST PEOPLE
In the 1970s, strange items (left) appeared on the antiques market. Scholars investigated them and tracked down a whole new culture, which had flourished in Bactria in 2500-1500 B.C. The Bactrians were wealthy traders who controlled the land route between the Indus Valley and Mesopotamia.

One clue to a people's identity is their language. One ancient language was Proto-Indo-European. Over the centuries, the groups who spoke it began to drift apart. They traveled across Europe and into the Middle East, then on to India and Turkestan. Each group changed its language so much that they would not have been able to communicate if they had met. The family of languages now called Indo-European includes almost all European languages, Russian, Ukranian, Armenian, Iranian and most of the major languages of India and Pakistan, as well as many ancient languages.

HITTITE CONQUESTS
By 2000 B.C., the Hittites had arrived in Anatolia from north of the Black Sea. They gradually established an empire and a writing system (below). At first they were Egypt's enemies, but then they sealed a treaty. They were wiped out by the Sea Peoples (see page 163).

Brutal invaders... or peaceful settlers?
Because their victims wrote all the known records of their actions, the Vikings have been regarded as pirates for centuries. Some were, but most were farmers and skilled craftspeople. Others were daring merchants who traveled as far as the Middle East. There were also intrepid explorers who founded colonies in Russia, Iceland, Greenland, and North America.

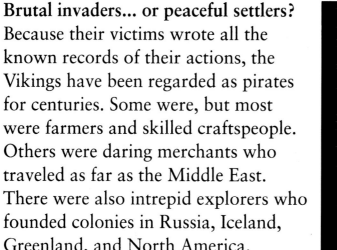

THE FIRST MINOANS

In about 6000 B.C., the ancestors of the Minoans arrived on the island of Crete, probably from Anatolia. Archeologists have traced their progress from simple farmers to a great trading nation. They invented their own writing system, which we call Linear A, but as yet no one can read it. Linear B, the writing of the later Mycenaeans (see page 162), is readable because it was an early form of Greek, which is an Indo-European language.

THE ROSE-RED CITY

In the fourth century B.C., an Arab tribe, the Nabataeans, set up a kingdom in what had been Edom. They controlled the trade routes from Arabia and the Red Sea to the Mediterranean, and became rich and powerful. Their great capital, Petra, was built of a pinkish stone and surrounded by cliffs. Its entrance was a narrow cleft in the rocks, while its temples and tombs were cut into the cliffs. It came under Roman rule in 106 A.D., and gradually declined.

THE MISSING MARVELS OF ANGKOR

The Khmers of Cambodia expanded their empire after A.D. 800 and built a great temple complex at Angkor Wat and a capital at Angkor Thom. But the Thais defeated them in the early 1400s and their buildings were lost in the jungle. They were found by chance, by Henri Mouhot in 1860.

What is the oldest alphabet?
The earliest writing systems used hieroglyphs (pictures) rather than letters. The Phoenician system was then adapted by the ancient Greeks into the first alphabet. The letter O is thought to be the most ancient written letter. We know it was used as early as 1300 B.C. – and it has not changed its shape since.

"*Moreover, all this ruin was brought upon the Romans by a woman, a fact which in itself caused them the greatest shame.*"

Cassius Dio of Rome, writing over 100 years after Boudicca's revolt

Missing PEOPLE

A society may record the deeds of its great men and women, but over time the texts can be lost or destroyed. Our knowledge about them is therefore limited, but there is always hope that an excavation will find more texts!

If the few accounts of an event are written by one side only, they are likely to be biased. The British revolt of A.D. 60-61, led by Queen Boudicca of the Iceni tribe, is a good example. It killed thousands of Roman colonists and soldiers, important towns were destroyed and Rome nearly lost its new land. But the Romans won in the end and wrote of a struggle of law, order, and civilization against savagery and ignorance. Boudicca and the Britons who died were portrayed as fierce and unworthy. If the Iceni had kept records, they might have written of their heroic struggle to drive out invaders whose greed, cruelty, and brutal treatment of Queen Boudicca had made them unworthy of being treated with honor or mercy.

The Forgotten WOMEN

Our knowledge about women in history is limited. This is partly due to destruction of records over time, and partly because some societies were ruled by men who believed women were of little importance and so denied them any rights or power outside the home. The records of such a culture give few details about women. If a male-dominated society was threatened by a woman, its writers usually did their best to blacken her name. We can find many "lost" women through texts and excavations, but we must be very careful not to be fooled by the attitudes of the authors of the texts!

How did Queen Boudicca die?
After her defeat, in A.D. 61, Boudicca committed suicide rather than being taken prisoner by the Romans. Records say that the Iceni gave her a costly burial, but it is not clear where. Several places in Britain claim the honor of being the site of the queen's last resting place. One theory says that she lies under Platform 8 of London's King's Cross railroad station! Will this mystery ever be solved?

A KING WITH A DIFFERENCE
Women were honored in ancient Egypt but only a man could ascend to the throne. A few women got around this rule. Queen Hatshepsut claimed that the god Amun had chosen her to rule and reigned as "King." After her death, her nephew destroyed her monuments to remove all traces of her. Archaeologists are now defeating him by putting the pieces back together again!

PAYING THE PRICE
Zenobia, Queen of Palmyra, in Syria, carved her own empire by conquering Rome's eastern provinces. When she was finally defeated, the Romans tried to humiliate her by making her walk in the emperor's victory parade – but she had the last laugh. She married a senator and became a famous hostess!

168

THE MYSTERIOUS QUEEN

Nefertiti was the wife of Akhenaten (see page 163). After their deaths, their enemies tried to destroy all records of their religious revolution, leaving us with many questions. Did Nefertiti support her husband's worship of Aten? Did she become "King" for a while? When and how did she die?

THE MOST FAMOUS QUEEN IN HISTORY

Our information about Queen Cleopatra VII comes mainly from Roman records. She had scared the Romans by helping Mark Antony to fight against Octavian (later Emperor Augustus). She was a good ruler, but the Roman writers described her as unworthy.

THE LEGEND OF SHEBA

The Bible tells how the Queen of Sheba learned of the wisdom of King Solomon and went to visit him. In fact, Sheba's kingdom was rich from trade. She and Solomon were probably making a trade deal!

BURIED IN STATE

Wonderfully preserved in an intricate tomb, surrounded by treasures and wrapped in beautiful silks, a mysterious Chinese noblewoman was discovered by archaeologists in the 1980s. Modern medical techniques have shown the illnesses she suffered from and how she passed her last hours.

A scandal in Rome

Legend says that a young woman once disguised herself as a man and was elected Pope (the head of the Catholic Church)! She was nicknamed "Pope Joan." The story may have arisen because in the tenth century A.D. there were some very weak Popes. A mother and daughter called Theodora and Marozia gained influence over several of them, even deciding who the new Popes should be!

People of LEGEND

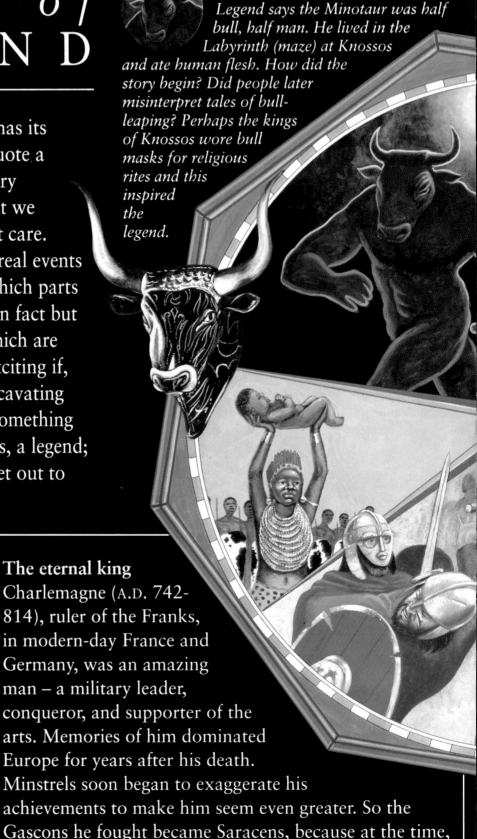

THE BEAST IN THE LABYRINTH
Legend says the Minotaur was half bull, half man. He lived in the Labyrinth (maze) at Knossos and ate human flesh. How did the story begin? Did people later misinterpret tales of bull-leaping? Perhaps the kings of Knossos wore bull masks for religious rites and this inspired the legend.

Every country and culture has its legends. It is tempting to quote a legend to help prove a theory about a piece of history, but we must use legends with great care. A legend may be based on real events but it is not always clear which parts are true, which are based on fact but have been changed, and which are later additions. It can be exciting if, while studying a text or excavating a site, archaeologists find something that fits in with, or explains, a legend; but they do not normally set out to prove that a legend is true.

The eternal king
Charlemagne (A.D. 742-814), ruler of the Franks, in modern-day France and Germany, was an amazing man – a military leader, conqueror, and supporter of the arts. Memories of him dominated Europe for years after his death. Minstrels soon began to exaggerate his achievements to make him seem even greater. So the Gascons he fought became Saracens, because at the time, the Saracens were Europe's greatest enemy. It was even said that he was not dead but would return to rule one day.

RIDING THROUGH THE GLEN

England's best-loved folk hero is Robin Hood... but who was he? Over the centuries, writers have altered his identity to suit the views of the time – from a peasant to an earl!

Was Robin Hood one man, or did the deeds of several outlaws get credited to one person? Legend places Robin in the reign of King Richard I (1189-1199), but an outlaw called Robin Hood is recorded as living later. Did he use the name of the earlier outlaw, or was he the real one?

A TERRIBLE SACRIFICE

When civil war raged in 18th-century West Africa, legend says that Queen Pokou and her people fled, but reached a vast, swiftly-flowing river. In return for a safe crossing, the gods demanded the sacrifice of a child. Pokou could have killed a poor woman's child, but she sacrificed her own son.

Do legend and reality ever get mixed up? Myth and fact often become confused as a story is passed down through the centuries. For example, legend says that an early Count of Anjou, in France, met a beautiful girl called Melusine in a forest. He fell in love, married her and they lived happily – until he found out that she was the daughter of the Devil! Melusine's descendants are said to include England's Plantagenet kings (1154-1399), the ancestors of today's British royal family.

WARRIOR WOMEN

Greek writers told how Mycenaean heroes fought the Amazons, a tribe of women, who went to what is now Russia. Scholars dismissed the stories, but in the 1950s archaeologists found the graves of a nomadic tribe in Russia. Some women's graves contained weapons and armor of the right date for the Amazons.

ROUND TABLE RIDDLES

Who was the real King Arthur? Early texts suggest he was a Roman Briton who fought the Saxons. Details like the sword Excalibur, his knights and the Round Table came later. When the Saxons won, some Britons fled to Wales, where bards reworked the story. Medieval minstrels, 15th-century poets, and Victorian writers added to it, creating the legend as it is today.

"*Whether you like it or not,
history is on our side.
We will bury you!*"

Nikita Khrushchev, President of the
former U.S.S.R., in a speech to
Western ambassadors, 1956

Mysterious OBJECTS

Considering the destruction caused by time, nature, and people, an amazing number of buildings, texts, and objects have survived! But these represent only a tiny fraction of the glories of past civilizations. A site can be destroyed and completely lost if we have no references to it in any texts.

Texts mention many places, but we do not know where they were. Some are found by careful investigation. Sometimes we know where a city was but it is difficult to get at – the ruins of Pompeii, for example. The Romans destroyed the city of Carthage, in North Africa, but thanks to careful excavation archaeologists are finding out about Rome's great rival and know what its magnificent harbor (left) and splendid docks were like.

Some people just cannot resist a challenge! They continue to search for objects and places that most scholars believe no longer exist, such as biblical objects like Noah's Ark and the Ark of the Covenant.

The Lost
B O O K S

It is bad enough when books and the vital information they hold are destroyed by accident. It is awful if they are tampered with to fit the ideas of the day. But history is littered with instances of the deliberate destruction of books. Many rulers have destroyed texts to erase the memory of enemies or burned books to stop the spread of "unacceptable" ideas.

One of the greatest thrills for an archaeologist is to find a text with vital historical information. Such a find was the Turin Papyrus, which gave a full list of Egypt's kings. The papyrus was so badly damaged during transport that experts are still trying to piece it back together again.

Have ancient writings influenced our lives? We owe a lot to the wisdom of the past, which has come to us via the Greeks and Romans. The Egyptians invented the 365-day calender and divided the day into 24 hours. The Babylonians used a system of numbers based on 60, from which we get 360 degrees in a circle, 60 minutes in an hour, and 60 seconds in a minute.

THE LOSS OF A LONG HISTORY
The Maya and Aztecs made scrolls of bark or deerskin covered with pictures of their past. The Spaniards burned most of them and had a new one, the Codex Mendoza, *made, showing Aztec daily life.*

MISSING RECORDS
The Library of Alexandria held about 500,000 books and scholars came from far and wide to read them. Part of it was burned down during Caesar's campaign in Egypt (48 B.C.). The rest was destroyed in the A.D. 270s. Think of all the historical information we have lost!

FATAL OPINIONS
In 221 B.C., Cheng, the ruler of Qin province, became the emperor of all China. When he heard that some scholars were criticizing him, he ordered the burning of all books, old and new, that might be used against him. Later he had 460 scholars executed.

The Dead Sea scrolls
In 1947, a shepherd boy found a cave at Qumran, on the shores of the Dead Sea. It contained some strange, ancient scrolls. Over the next few years, other caves and scrolls were discovered. The study of these texts was held up by scholarly, political, and religious rivalry, but they are now becoming available. The scrolls contain biblical texts, writings about the Bible, calendars, and hymns. They date from the first centuries B.C. and A.D. and were probably hidden during the Jewish revolts of A.D. 66 and 132, to save them from the Romans. They tell us about religious life before the birth of Christ and so are important to Christians, Jews, and Muslims alike.

THE SECRET GOSPELS
In the early days of Christianity, there were many different Christian groups. The Gnostics claimed to have secret knowledge, so the Church had their writings destroyed. One Gnostic buried his books at Nag Hammadi in Egypt. They were found by a farmer a few years ago!

WORDS OF WISDOM
A Sibyl was a Roman prophetess (a woman who could foresee the future). One Sibyl sold three books of her writings to King Tarquinius of Rome. The Sibylline prophecies were said to be very accurate and were consulted in times of trouble. They were destroyed by fire in 83 B.C., so we will never know how accurate they were.

Why Were They M A D E ?

People in the past were prepared to go to great lengths to make and build things, using up vast amounts of time and energy (when lives were much shorter than today). What made Stone Age hunters, who needed all their energy to survive in an Ice Age, go deep into caves to produce wonders like the Lascaux paintings (see page 178)? It is often difficult to work out how and why things were made. For example, some people still find it hard to believe that so much effort went into building Egypt's pyramids simply for them to be used as tombs. When we have no texts, just objects or ruins, it is even more difficult to interpret them.

Were old towns like modern ones?
In the town of Çatal Hüyük (in what is now Turkey), one of the first towns in the world, there were no roads and the houses were entered through a hole in the roof! The town had wide trading links and was very rich. Its citizens may have feared that jealous neighboring towns might try to attack them.

THE STANDING STONES
The peoples of Bronze Age Europe (3500-1000 B.C.) have left behind many monuments made of menhirs (upright stones). Some are in long lines; others are in circles. The most famous circle is Stonehenge (left) in southern England. Clearly it was built for religious rites, perhaps related to the Sun, as it faces the midsummer rising and midwinter setting of the Sun. But what about the stones with human faces on the island of Corsica (top)? Do they represent gods, heroes, or enemies?

AN EVERLASTING MEMORIAL
Native Americans built the Rock Eagle Effigy Mound in A.D. 500. Its wingspan is 120 ft (36 m). This is one of many monuments left by cultures that flourished from 1000 B.C. to A.D. 1500 in the Ohio and Mississippi river valleys.

Many built mounds. Some were for burials or had palaces on top. Others must have had religious use, but without written evidence we can only guess at it.

MYSTERIOUS MONUMENTS

Easter Island is only 15.5 miles (26 km) long, yet between A.D. 600 and 1500, its Polynesian people carved about 1,000 huge stone heads. Were they to honor great ancestors? Civil war and famine meant that statue building ceased.

PICTURES IN THE SAND

The Nazca people flourished along the south coast of Peru from about 200 B.C. to A.D. 600. They made lines across the desert by clearing away the stones and exposing the sand. Some of the lines are several miles long, some form patterns, and others depict huge monkeys, spiders, and birds. Were they drawn to please gods in the sky?

Guardians of the dead

Models of servants were placed in the graves of early Chinese kings and nobles, but the First Emperor (221-210 B.C.) outdid them all! In his tomb at Mount Li, a whole army, sculpted in terracotta, was buried. Over 8,000 life-sized models have been found so far. Most are foot soldiers, but there are also horses, chariots, and officers. Three attempts had been made on Cheng's life. He must have wanted a safe afterlife, guarded by his most trusted warriors.

LAWS OF STONE

King Asoka of India (272-231 B.C.) set up this pillar (right) to mark the spot where the Buddha first taught. Writings on many other pillars across India told of Asoka's laws to encourage peace and happiness in his land.

THE FIRST EGYPTIAN DAM

Recent excavations in Egypt have found that, in about 2600 B.C., the Egyptians were building a dam to protect villages from floods rushing down a narrow valley. But a flood destroyed the dam before it was completed.

"Treasure hunting is as old as Man; scientific archaeology is a modern development, but in its short life... it has done marvels."

Sir Leonard Woolley, *Digging up the Past*, 1940

New Ideas and INVESTIGATIONS

Archaeologists are leading the battle to find the lost treasures of the past. Their excavations are still uncovering hidden objects, buildings, texts, cities, and even entire civilizations. Historians and language experts then analyze the material. Unlike the archaeologists of the past, today's researchers are able to call upon specialized scientists and the latest modern technology to help them.

Archaeology is now more popular than ever before. Books and TV programs have made it exciting, and air travel means that thousands of people can now visit the world's wonders. This is great for tourism, but it can also cause archaeological problems. Too many people walking over sites can destroy the very things they have come to see! The caves at Lascaux, France, have been closed since 1963. While they were open to visitors, algae had entered the caves. It spread rapidly and began to destroy the 17,000-year-old paintings (left).

Faces from THE PAST

All historians dream about how wonderful it would be to meet people from the past, and, very occasionally, this dream almost comes true. Ancient Egyptians mummified their dead, so we have the thrill of looking at the faces of some of the pharaohs and their subjects. Sometimes natural conditions have preserved ancient bodies and faces in an excellent condition. Archaeologists can also turn to the modern police technique of rebuilding a face over the bones of a skull. Experts use clay to build up the muscles, tissues, and features such as the nose and mouth, until an ancient face looks out at them once again.

THE FACE OF PHILIP
In 1977, archaeologists found what they believed was the tomb of the Macedonian king Philip II, but they had no proof. An expert built up a clay face over the skull found in the tomb. It belonged to a man aged 40-50, with a scar over his right eye. We know Philip was wounded (and probably blinded) by an arrow in his eye – so it must be his tomb.

The Ice Man
One autumn day, about 5,000 years ago, a man was trudging through the Alps of Austria when he was caught in a blizzard. He lay down to sleep, and never awoke. His body, preserved by the ice, was found in 1991. We are getting valuable information about life in his time from his possessions. But why was he all alone? Was he a trader, a shepherd, or a priest? Had he left his village in a hurry?

BURIED IN THE BOG

The bogs of northern Europe have preserved many bodies, slain and thrown into the mud. We know that Iron Age people often made human sacrifices to their gods and goddesses. Were these bodies sacrificial victims? Some may have been criminals being punished or volunteers who hoped to bring luck to their tribe by pleasing the gods.

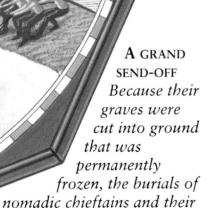

A GRAND SEND-OFF

Because their graves were cut into ground that was permanently frozen, the burials of nomadic chieftains and their families have been well preserved in the Altai Mountains of Kazakhstan. Objects of wood, cloth, and leather, sacrificed horses, and tattooed bodies have all survived since 400-200 B.C.

VICTIMS OF VESUVIUS

In A.D. 79, Mount Vesuvius in Italy erupted and the city of Pompeii was buried by ash and pumice stone. Most of its inhabitants fled, but those who stayed were suffocated by fumes. Their bodies decayed, but the ash hardened around them, preserving their impressions. By filling the hollows with plaster, archaeologists can make replicas of the ancient bodies.

A GAZE FROM THE PAST

She lived in ancient Egypt and was about 14 when she died. Her mummy was reduced to bones. She suffered from a nose complaint and had lost both legs from the knee down, but we do not know if this happened before or after her death. This mysterious girl's face has been rebuilt on her skull and even given makeup.

THE FACE OF A KING

Timur Leng (Timur the Lame, 1336-1405), known in the West as Tamerlane, carved an empire in the Middle East and Central Asia. When historians opened his tomb, they asked experts to build up the face over the skull they found. It revealed the strong character of the ruthless warlord!

What can modern medicine tell us about people of the past?
Medical knowledge can help historians greatly. Most statues of Alexander the Great show him with his chin in the air and his head to one side. People thought it showed his arrogance. Recently, two doctors have suggested that he may have had a rare eye disease called Brown's Syndrome. The only way for sufferers to see properly is to hold their head in the way shown in the statues.

Methods of the FUTURE

Science, technology, medicine – all have made rapid progress over the last few years, greatly helping scholars and archaeologists. There are new techniques to help them find things and others to help them date those that they find. They can reconstruct an ancient landscape by finding and analyzing pollen and tiny organisms from a site. Medical techniques can now reveal more about ancient bodies and analyze blood and DNA. Science can help to conserve things better than ever and to detect fakes, too – forgers, beware!

WHAT LIES BELOW?
Opening and examining tombs take time and money. Archaeologists use special equipment to detect underground hollows in some areas. If a tomb is found, a hole is drilled and a camera put in. Photos are taken to see if it is worth opening.

Do people ever fake ancient finds?
The skull of "Piltdown Man," found in 1912, was hailed as a "missing link" in evolution. In 1953, it was proved to be a fake. An old trunk was found that belonged to a curator at the Natural History Museum, in London, England, at the time. It is stained with the same chemicals as those used by the hoaxer!

THE PRIDE OF THE FLEET
The Mary Rose sank in 1545 near Plymouth, England. She settled on the seabed, where silt preserved one half. Raised in 1982, she is providing valuable details about Tudor life and ship-building.

VIRTUAL HISTORY
Have you ever looked at ruins and wondered what the original building was like? Thanks to computers, you can now find out. Plans of a ruin can be used to produce a 3-D reconstruction. You can see the building as its original occupants knew it.

Aerial archaeology

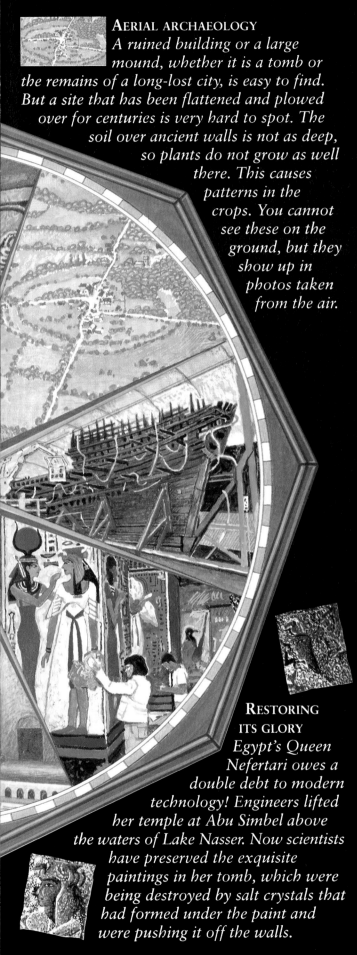

A ruined building or a large mound, whether it is a tomb or the remains of a long-lost city, is easy to find. But a site that has been flattened and plowed over for centuries is very hard to spot. The soil over ancient walls is not as deep, so plants do not grow as well there. This causes patterns in the crops. You cannot see these on the ground, but they show up in photos taken from the air.

Happy families

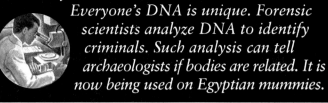

DNA is a substance in our body, inherited from both our parents. It determines how we look. Everyone's DNA is unique. Forensic scientists analyze DNA to identify criminals. Such analysis can tell archaeologists if bodies are related. It is now being used on Egyptian mummies.

Underwater magic

World War II (1939-1945) saw the development of the Aqua-Lung, which allows divers to swim and use their arms freely. This led to the birth of marine archaeology. Dozens of shipwrecks have yielded up details of their cargoes and the secrets of their construction. Buildings drowned by the sea may also be excavated. Blocks from the lighthouse at Alexandria have been found recently, with statues that once adorned the city.

Restoring its glory

Egypt's Queen Nefertari owes a double debt to modern technology! Engineers lifted her temple at Abu Simbel above the waters of Lake Nasser. Now scientists have preserved the exquisite paintings in her tomb, which were being destroyed by salt crystals that had formed under the paint and were pushing it off the walls.

What next?

We have yet to identify Helen of Troy, Robin Hood remains hidden in the Greenwood, and Arthur is still the "once and future" King. There are lost people, treasures, cities, and civilizations to be found and new tools with which to find them. For archaeologists, the past has an exciting future. You can enjoy it, too.

TIME

c. 15,000 B.C. *Lascaux cave paintings are made*

c. 3100-30 B.C. *Egypt flourishes*
c. 3000-1450 B.C. *Minoan civilization*

c. 2950-1500 B.C. *Stonehenge built, England*
c. 2600 B.C. *First Egyptian dam started*
c. 2500-1700 B.C. *Civilization in Indus Valley*
c. 2500-1500 B.C. *Bactrian culture at its peak*
c. 2000 B.C. *Hittites arrive in Anatolia (Turkey)*

c. 1900-1000 B.C. *Mycenaean civilization flourishes*
c. 1450 B.C. *Santorini volcano destroys Minoans*
c. 1367-1350 B.C. *Akhenaton rules Egypt*
c. 1190 B.C. *"Sea Peoples" defeat Hittites*
c. 1000 B.C.-A.D. *1500 Native American cultures flourish in Ohio & Mississippi river valleys*

c. 800 B.C.-A.D. *100 Greek civilization*
c. 753 B.C.-A.D. *476 Roman civilization*
c. 612 B.C. *City of Babylon rebuilt*
c. 550 B.C.-A.D. *350 Meroe at its peak*
c. 432 B.C. *Statue of Zeus built at Olympia*
400s B.C.-A.D. *200s Petra is an important city*
c. 280 B.C. *Lighthouse at Alexandria built*
c. 272-231 B.C. *King Asoka rules India*
c. 221-210 B.C. *Cheng rules China*
c. 200 B.C.-A.D. *600 Nazca lines are created*
c. 83 B.C. *Sibylline prophesies are destroyed*
51-30 B.C. *Cleopatra* VII *rules Egypt*

A.D. *60-62 Queen Boudicca leads British revolt against Romans*
66 B.C. *&* A.D. *132 Jewish revolts against Roman rule*
A.D. *79 Town of Pompeii destroyed by eruption of Mount Vesuvius*

LINE

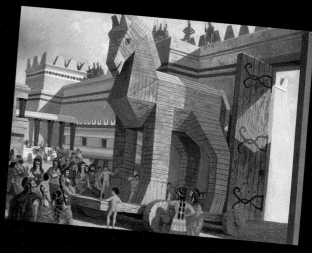

A.D. **270s** Library of Alexandria is destroyed
A.D. **462** Statue of Zeus destroyed
A.D. **476** Roman Empire falls
c. A.D. **500** Rock Eagle Mound collapses
A.D. **600s** King Arthur thought to exist
A.D. **600-1500** Easter Island statues erected
A.D. **800s** Khmers build Angkor Wat & Thom

1336-1405 Timur Leng (Tamerlane) lives
1375 Lighthouse at Alexandria is destroyed
1521-1522 Tenochtitlan destroyed by the Spaniards
1545 The Mary Rose sinks off the English coast
1748-present Excavations at Pompeii & neighboring town of Herculaneum, Italy
1843 John Stephens finds Chichén Itzá
1870 Heinrich Schliemann finds Troy
1876 Schliemann excavates Mycenae
1893-1935 Arthur Evans finds Minoan remains
1911 Hiram Bingham finds Machu Picchu
1912 "Piltdown Man" bones discovered (but are proved to be a hoax in 1953)
1922 Howard Carter opens tomb of King Tutankhamen; Leonard Woolley excavates Ur
1940 Schoolboys find Lascaux cave paintings
1945-1948 Mortimer Wheeler excavates Indus Valley
1947 Dead Sea scrolls found in cave at Qumran
1974 Tomb of First Emperor discovered, China
1977 Tomb of Philip II of Macedonia discovered
1980s Examination of Chinese noblewoman
1991 Frozen man – "Ötzi" – discovered in glacier in Austrian mountains
1992 Minoan paintings discovered in ancient Egyptian tombs
1995 Tomb containing over 50 sons of King Ramses II discovered in Egypt
1996 Tomb of Queen Nefetari reopened

GLOSSARY

Adobe – Unfired mud-brick, dried in the sun.

Ammonite – A fossil with a large spiral shape; abundant in the Triassic era.

Amphibian – Backboned animal that lives on dry land, but must return to the water to breed.

Anubis – The Egyptian guardian of the dead.

Apollo 11 – The spacecraft which took Neil Armstrong and "Buzz" Aldrin to the Moon on July 20, 1969. They were the first two men to set foot on the Moon.

Aquaculture – When seas, lakes, and ponds are used for fish-farming, shellfish cultivation, and growing plants.

Aqua-Lung – A compressed air tank, used for breathing when underwater diving.

Archaeology – The study of ancient remains and artifacts.

Artifact – Object made by a person a long time ago, like a tool or a piece of art.

Asteroid – A huge chunk of rock that orbits between the planets.

Astrology – The study of the stars, planets, and constellations; which is based on the belief that the stars control life.

Atmosphere – A layer of gaseous air which surrounds the Earth and various other planets. The gases begin to deplete around 60 miles above ground level.

Aurora – A huge glowing wave of light in the sky over the North and South Poles. These lights form when particles of solar wind, from the Sun, hits the Earth's magnetic field.

Basilica – A large ancient Roman building, used as a town hall or law court.

Bathyscaph – An underwater observation vehicle.

Black holes – A field with such a strong gravitational pull that matter and energy cannot escape.

Canopic jar – A vase in the shape of a human head, which holds the internal organs of a mummified person.

Coelacanth – An ancient breed of fish.

Comet – A luminous heavenly body with a fiery tail, having a very unusual orbit.

Constellation – A group of stars.

Cryogenics – A branch of physics which is concerned with very low temperatures.

Decompression sickness – An illness that affects divers when they ascend too fast and are subjected to decreased pressure.

DNA – The hereditary material which makes up genes.

Eclipse – A cutting off of light which occurs when the Moon partially or totally hides the Sun from the Earth.

Embalming – Preserving a dead body with aromatic drugs.

Era – An interval of geological time, comprising of several periods.

Evolution – A gradual change in the characteristics of a population of animals or plants over many generations. The evolutionary theory is that all plants and animals are related to a single common ancestor.

Extinction – An ending, or annihilation of something; no longer found; i.e. the dinosaurs.

Fossil – Remains, of a plant or animal that once lived, usually found embedded in rock and earth.

Galaxy – A great band of stars traveling through space.

Gene – The unit of hereditary information which passes characteristics from parents to offspring.

Genetics – The branch of biology that focuses on heredity, DNA, and physical variations of organisms.

Gill – The "breathing" parts of a fish, which does the same job as the lungs of a land animal. Gills are designed to extract oxygen dissolved in the water. They are usually feathery, blood-rich parts located behind the head.

Hieroglyphics – The ancient Egyptian method of writing, using pictures and symbols.

Huaca – Places or objects regarded as holy by the Incas and their subjects.

Ice Age – A period of time during which a large part of the Earth's surface was covered with ice.

Inundation – The annual flooding of the Nile river which provided farmers with fertile, silty soil.

Libation – An ancient Greek offering of wine poured over an altar during worship of the gods.

Mammal – The highest class of vertebrate, including humans; they are warm blooded, have hairy bodies, and can produce milk for their young.

Marsupial – A primitive mammal that gives birth to underdeveloped offspring and raises them in a pouch, such as a kangaroo or a possum.

Mastaba – An ancient Egyptian tomb with slanted sides and a flat top, used for burial purposes.

Mermaids – A mythical sea creature with the tail of a fish and the top half of a woman.

Mestizo – Person of mixed European and American Indian descent.

Meteorite – A Large mass of matter that has shot through the atmosphere and fallen to the Earth's surface.

Milky Way – Earth's galaxy, which contains approximately 100,000 million stars.

Minoan – The name given to the civilization that flourished on Crete from around 2000-1450 B.C.

Minotaur – In legend, a monster who was half-man, half-bull and lived in the labyrinth on Crete.

Mollusk – An unsegmented, shelled invertebrate, that possesses a single muscular foot which is used for digging.

Moon – An object in space which orbits a larger object, usually a planet.

Mosaic – A pattern or picture made of tiny pieces of tile or glass.

Mummy – A dead body which has been preserved by embalming.

Mycenaean – The name given to the people who dominated mainland Greece from about 1600-1200 B.C.

Myth – An old traditional story or legend concerning fabulous or supernatural beings.

Nahuatl – The language of the Aztecs; in contemporary Mexico it is spoken by around 1.4 million people.

Nova – A star which suddenly increases in brilliance.

Oracle – A shrine where people could consult a god or goddess who spoke to them through a priest or priestess.

Orbit – The oval shaped path of one object traveling around another.

Paleontologist – Someone who studies fossils.

Pangaea – A great land mass or super-continent, which existed over 200 million years ago.

Papyrus – A material for writing on, made out of reeds.

Pearl – A secretion of calcium carbonate formed around an irritant (a grain of sand), produced by some mollusks.

Pharaoh – A very powerful king in ancient Egypt, after about 1554 B.C. – pharaohs were sometimes thought to be gods.

Piltdown Man – A fake specimen of the first "intellegent" human, consisting of a human skull and an ape jaw.

Planet – A relatively large object that orbits a star.

Primate – A monkey, ape, or human; a mammal with a large brain, good eyesight, and flexible hands.

Reptiles – A group of animals that are scaly, land-living, and backboned, such as turtles, snakes, and crocodiles.

Rosetta stone – A tablet found in Egypt in 1799 which was inscribed with hieroglyphs, demotic script, and Greek. It became the key to deciphering ancient Egyptian hieroglyphs.

Satellite – An object in space that orbits a larger object, usually refers to an artificial, or man-made, space object.

SCUBA – Self-Contained Underwater Breathing Apparatus.

Skeleton – The structure, made from bones, which forms the framework for a body, supporting the muscles.

Solar System – A collection of planets that orbit a star. The Earth's solar system has a total of nine planets that move around the Sun.

Sonar – An apparatus which locates a submerged object by emitting high-frequency sound waves.

Species – A group of plants or animals that normally interbreed successfully. All members of a species look similar.

Sphinx – A creature from Greek mythology, which was half-woman, half-lioness. It was believed to ask riddles to travelers, and then kill those who could not answer them.

Sun – The star which the Earth's solar system orbits.

Supernova – Extremely bright nova, resulting from an explosion that scatters the star's contents into space.

Tectonic plates – Rigid plates which make up the Earth's surface, or lithosphere.

Telescope – An optical device used for seeing objects at a great distance; mostly used to look into space.

Temple – A building used for the worship of a god.

UFO – An Unidentified Flying Object.

Ufology – The study of UFOs.

Universe – The cosmos; including all galaxies, stars, planets, and space.

Vertebrate – An animal with a backbone. Vertebrates are a large group that includes fish, amphibians, reptiles, birds, and mammals.

Volcano – A rift or vent in the Earth's crust through which molten material, or lava, is ejected. Volcanoes were feared as gods by many ancient peoples.

Whirlpool – A circular current in a body of water, caused by meeting currents, wind, or the shape of the body.

Wormholes – A short cut or link between one point in space-time and another.

X ray – A photograph that enables people to study the details of objects invisible to the naked eye.

Ziggurat – A temple-like structure, built with a series of mastabas, one on top of the other, decreasing in size as they go upward.

INDEX

Photocredits:

Ancient Art & Architecture Collection; Bruce Coleman Collection; Frank Spooner Pictures; York Archaeological Trust; Mary Evans Picture Library; James Davis Travel Photography; Science Photo Library; NASA; Robert Harding Picture Library; Hulton Deutsch; Courtesy of the Trustees of the British Museum, London; Eye Ubiquitous; Courtesy of Rudolf Ganbrink; Roger Vlitos; Hutchison Library; Spectrum Colour Library